NOISE FROM THE
WRITING CENTER

NOISE FROM THE WRITING CENTER

ELIZABETH H. BOQUET

UTAH STATE
UNIVERSITY PRESS
Logan, Utah

Utah State University Press
Logan, Utah 84322-7800

Manufactured in the United States of America.
Cover design by Sans Serif.
Cover photo: *If 6 Was 9*, by Trimpin. Courtesy of the Experience Music Project. All rights reserved

Library of Congress Cataloging-in-Publication Data

Boquet, Elizabeth, 1966-
  Noise from the writing center / Elizabeth Boquet.
    p. cm.
  Includes bibliographical references and index.
  ISBN 0-87421-434-3 (alk. paper)
  1. English language—Rhetoric—Study and teaching. 2. Report
writing—Study and teaching (Higher) 3. Tutors and tutoring. 4.
Writing centers. I. Title.
  PE1404 .B66 2002
  808'.042'0711—dc21

2001007759

To my mom and dad,
for music lessons, play practices,
and *Green Eggs and Ham*

CONTENTS

ACKNOWLEDGMENTS

Writing this book has often felt, to use Annie Lamott's delicious phrase, "like putting an octopus to bed." Like noise, a flailing limb is a signal, a sign frequently of distress, but also an expression of hope, of possible freedom and of rescue.

I have experienced all of this while putting these ideas on paper, and it is here that I wish to acknowledge those people who have rescued me, in all sorts of ways, during the time I've spent thinking, writing, and living. Though this list may seem long to those who read it, it is short to me, knowing as I do how many others, whose names do not appear here, have also sustained me.

Thanks to my friends and colleagues on *Wcenter*, in the International Writing Centers Association, and in the Northeast Writing Centers Association, who brought me into the writing center fold as a graduate student and whose dedication, humor, and commitment to this work I value especially.

To those writing center colleagues who have become treasured friends, especially Pete Gray, Neal Lerner, Anne Geller, Michele Eodice, and Libby Miles. You remind me that this work is supposed to be challenging *and* fun. And you make it so. To Ben Rafoth, who made the writing center at Indiana University of Pennsylvania a place I wanted to hang out, as well as a place I wanted to work. To Nancy Welch, for her theorizing about writing center work and writing center play.

To my graduate school compadres from IUP, especially Margie Vagt, Shelly Orr, Ann Ott, Gail Tayko, John Tassoni, Nancy Leech, and Todd Krug, for conversations about teaching and writing and researching that moved out of our classrooms and wound up around the tables of our Women's Dinners and under the clear evening skies of Two Lick Reservoir.

To my colleagues at Fairfield, from whom I continue to learn about the teaching/research/service triad by their personal and professional examples, especially John Thiel, Kathy Nantz, Dennis Keenan, and Betsy Bowen. To Susan Rakowitz, whose insistence on lunch provided much-needed breaks and sustenance. To David Schmidt, whose intellectual vision is equaled only by his knowledge of music/Hendrix/feedback/noise; and to Mariann Regan, who not only assumed the role of writing center director during much of the writing of this draft, but who actually enjoyed it.

To the peer tutors, whose takes on tutoring never fail to delight and surprise me. To the tutors at Fairfield University, whose minidramas and humorous renditions of campus life have made it difficult to sit in my office and write, even as they have given me so much to write about. To the tutors at Rhode Island College, without whom I am not sure I could have written this book. And I am quite sure it would not have been nearly as much fun. Thank you.

To Meg Carroll, for Zuka Juice, surf 'n' turf, bug zappers, and Water Fire. But mostly for her amazing program at Rhode Island College, as well as for unrestricted access to her copious notes, books, journals, tutors, laptops, videos, and mind.

To Mark Hurlbert and Michael Spooner, whose excitement about this project in all its incarnations has been unflagging and whose ideas about it always sent me back to write.

To my phantom limbs, the people in my life whose daily presence I miss most: Cristina Parsons and Geoff Sanborn, two former Fairfield colleagues and two of the dearest, smartest, funniest, most irreverent people I know; and my parents, my brother and his family—would that I could shrink the world.

To my husband, Dan Bedeker, for gently coaxing my sleeping limbs back to life. I promise longer bike rides and more frequent paddles through the marsh. Phew!

This work has also been supported in part by a Fairfield University Summer Research Stipend and by a grant from the National Writing Centers Association.

Despite all this assistance, there remain many shortcomings in this book. These are, of course, entirely my own.

"People ask me what music I listen to.
I listen to traffic and birds singing and people breathing.
And fire engines.
I always used to listen to the water pipes at night when the lights were
off,
and they played tunes.
Half the musical ideas I've had have been accidental."

John Lennon
(qtd. in Marzorati 31)

PROLOGUE

Being right can stop all the momentum of a very interesting idea.

Robert Rauschenberg (qtd. in Kimmelman 26)

We write only at the frontiers of our knowledge, at the border which separates our knowledge from our ignorance and transforms the one into the other. Only in this manner are we resolved to write.

Deleuze (xxi)

MEMORANDUM

Date:	October 20
To:	Dr. Beth Boquet
From:	PC
Subject:	Noise from the Writing Center

Since the Writing Center is located in the main Faculty Office Building, I would expect you and your staff to act with appropriate courtesy. I think it is inappropriate and discourteous to make such a racket as I heard coming from the Writing Center this evening. Even after I politely asked if the door could be closed, I again was interrupted by loud noises periodically coming from the Writing Center. When I politely mentioned this to James McMahon, who was working there, he acted as if I was somehow in the wrong to ask for quiet. Further, at no time did anyone apologize for making such a racket.

Faculty have an expectation that they can work in their offices with peace and quiet. The faculty office building is not an appropriate place for parties. I am deeply disappointed that you and your staff fail to recognize this, and would treat the faculty with such disrespect as I encountered this evening. I hope that you will speak to James in particular, and that you will do something about this problem to prevent its recurrence in the future.

MEMORANDUM

Date: October 21
To: Dr. PC
From: Beth Boquet
Subject: Noise in the Writing Center

I would like to take this opportunity to clear up what appear to be misunderstandings raised in your memo dated October 20.

1. The first stems from the assumption that the event to which you are referring was a party. It was in fact a writing center staff meeting, one aspect of the ongoing training that undergraduate peer tutors receive as part of their work in the Writing Center. It was attended by a total of seven people— five students and two faculty members. During Sunday night's hour-long meeting, we discussed successes and problems that tutors have encountered so far this semester, set up a system for staff communication (including a VAX Notes conference), and finalized a proposal that the tutors are submitting to the Northeast Writing Centers Association conference. I hope that from this partial list of the business conducted at Sunday's hour-long meeting, you can agree that it was not primarily a social gathering, but one where students were engaged in interesting academic work.

2. It is certainly arguable that Donnarumma Hall is, as you term it, the "main Faculty Office Building." As you are surely aware, office space and classroom space are shared in every building on this campus. I am well aware of the need to respect the working space of all members of the campus community, and I am frankly surprised that you would suggest otherwise. I would say, however, that this expectation must also extend to faculty's awareness that campus buildings, with the

possible exception of the library, are common spaces designed for intellectual engagement. This activity takes many forms, from individuals working in solitude to groups problem-solving collectively. I might also add that the deafening silence in most of our classroom buildings is a condition which I view to be a problem. The recent recommendations of the Dehne group [a campus marketing group who recommended, among other things, more visible collaborative student work spaces] support this conclusion.

3. This seems to be an issue primarily because the meeting was held on a Sunday, when we might expect there to be little activity in any of the buildings. I wonder if the same objections would have arisen had the meeting occurred at some other time. And I find it ironic that one of my primary considerations when scheduling these meetings is to select times that would prove least disruptive, say, for example, to Paul Lakeland [then-director of the Honors Program], who shares this office space with me, and to his students.

4. It also appears to be a problem that staff members, particularly James McMahon, were not appropriately deferential to you. I obviously cannot speak for James, nor will I presume to know what sort of exchange took place. I would like to point out that, in my opinion, a more appropriate channel might have been to speak to me directly. I am more than a bit confused as to why such an apparently simple matter has turned into this formal exchange.

I close by stating the obvious: Space on this campus is a huge problem. Ideally, the Writing Center would not be situated where it is. It is a space where people gather to talk and to share ideas. Ideally, faculty offices would be set apart from the main traffic of the building, as they are places where people often need privacy and solitude. This ideal is not our case. I and my staff will try to be more considerate in the future by closing the door. I expect that you will do the same by shutting yours. If this does not solve the problem, please let me know.

INTRODUCTION
Making a Joyful Noise

I ran into PC in the hall several days after the rapid-fire memo exchange you just read in the Prologue. He seemed somewhat mollified by my response. He admitted that he had been in the office late on a Sunday evening because he was struggling to meet the deadline for his tenure and promotion application—enough to put anyone in a bad mood. I understood. Things are fine.

But few moments in my professional life have nagged at me the way this moment nags at me. I consider it a profound irony that his memo, this piece of *writing*, which I found so momentarily devastating, has become instead so *productive* (like a dry, hacking cough that suddenly l-ooooo-sens up).

Nearly a decade before I met PC, in a writing center half a country away from the one in which I now work, I had my first devastating-yet-productive encounter, a meeting that shaped my response to PC, and my response to all things teaching- and writing-related, in important ways.

It was the fall of 1986. Todd[1] walked into the writing center where I was beginning my second year as a peer tutor. I imagine that moment now as characterized by the signs of self-deprecation that came to mark our sessions: his hunched shoulders, the slow shuffle of his feet, the slap of his notebook as it landed on the table. But I know I've imposed that reading on our initial encounter. I'm sure I thought there was nothing different about Todd when he sat with me that first morning. He was just another student attempting, on this, his third try, to pass the first course of the university's three-tiered basic writing sequence.

Three days a week we met, for a whole semester, following the dictates of the center, not working on his actual papers, but instead

conjugating the verb "to do" in the present tense and checking pro-
noun-antecedent agreement exercises and quizzing him on subordi-
nating and coordinating conjunctions. I imagine that we (or at least
I) began these sessions eagerly, sure that a semester's work in the
center would leave him a much better writer, and that we ended
them dejectedly, our heads in our hands, just trying to wade through
another frustrating day.

But like I said, I'm not sure that's the way it was.

What I do know for sure is that Todd failed the class. Again.

I don't know that our work together changed anything for him. At
least not for the better. I can't imagine that it did. But it changed a lot
for me—everything, in fact—sent me in search of answers about the
things I thought I knew, about the things he didn't know, about how
we both came to be where we were. I am bothered that Todd has
become another literate occasion for me, an event in *my* story, a story
that writes me farther and farther away from where we began, he and
I. But this is, in fact, the case: Todd made me feel no longer at home in
my home.

I am reluctant to read my work with Todd (and later my reaction to
PC's memo) as what Nancy Welch has called "a neat turning point,"
and I will follow her in viewing it instead as a moment that "worked to
disrupt continuity, development and unfolding," that "raised the dis-
comforting but revisionary questions: *What am I becoming? And What
else might I become?*" (1997, 31). My relationship with Todd presented
me with questions like these to ask about writing center work. I'm not
sure I even knew, before Todd, that there *were* questions to ask. I
thought my responsibility was simply to sit down and, well, just tutor.[2]
My work with Todd led directly, for me, to graduate school, to more
tutoring—this time in a writing center where questioning was modeled and valued—to a dissertation, and then to my decision to spend
my career working here, in a writing center of my own (so to speak).

For Todd, I can't say where our work led.

During the decade between Todd and PC, I learned a great deal,
and I often mentally revisited my work with Todd. As a beginning
tutor, I had imagined that there existed at least the possibility of perfect communication—no static, no noise—between a writer and a

text, between a tutor and a writer. Communication breakdowns were the fault of the receiver, hence my frustrating attempts to fine-tune first Todd's poor reception as a classroom student and later Todd's poor reception as a writing center client. Where he initially was failing at only one, he ended up failing at both. And knowing it.

My courses, my reading, and my writing in graduate school—I view them now largely as attempts to repair that faulty communication between Todd and me. I acknowledged some responsibility as sender for the failure of that communication, and I began to see myself—as tutor, as teacher—also as a *receiver* of information. My newfound awareness of the reciprocity between sender and receiver would, I was certain, draw me closer to that perfect session I should have had, but somehow managed never to have, with Todd. Other disruptions in that sender-receiver relationship came to the fore as I learned about the static, the noise, of the race-class-gender triad, and I refined my questions accordingly: What do we do with the static *in light of* the racial inequities in the educational system? How do we clean up the signal *in light of* the gender bias of the educational system? How do we restore *order* so that we can attempt *again* that perfect communication that we're somehow missing? The memo from PC stunned me into realizing that this was a whole lot of cleaning to do, and somehow it didn't seem right.

Coming a mere two years into my stint as a writing center director, the memo from PC left me, as I crafted my response, with the sickening suspicion that the entire project of perfect communication was somehow simply . . . doomed. Not in an hysterical, fleeting moment-of-sheer-panic kind-of-doomed, where you go to work a week or a month or a semester later and realize that oh-you-were-just-overreacting doomed. No. In a deep-seated, feel-it-in-my-bones, it's-too-early-in-my-career-for-me-to-feel-this-way kind of doomed.

Doom is such a depressing word. It even sounds heavy; it sits like a big thud on this page. Gloom. Loom. Doom. So I don't know how to explain, really, the energy I felt from that realization. It makes no sense, but there it is. I felt driven again, as I had with Todd, to think harder, smarter, differently. PC's memo made me think that maybe I had been asking the wrong questions, that maybe I needed to come up with a different set of questions, a different way of imagining the work of writing centers and the relationship of the work that goes on in them to students, to faculty, to . . . me.

This book begins, then, by considering what others have said about the work of writing centers and the relationships within them. Specifically, chapter one takes up the metaphors associated with writing center teaching, particularly the clinic and lab metaphors. Through this reconsideration, I try to make these metaphors more pliable, more flexible. In chapter two, I depart from previous metaphors associated with writing center work to consider a metaphor not so rooted in a politics of location, as are the clinic, lab, and center metaphors. I take up, instead, a metaphor of a more sonic nature: noise. I explore the relationship between noise and music in an attempt to hear again what tutors, students, and colleagues have been saying (and writing) about the institutional context of writing centers and about the pedagogical moments taking place in our writing centers (in other words, the feedback). In chapter three, I chronicle the summer 2000 staff education program at Rhode Island College, one that is suggestive of one direction that tutor education might move if we are to make hope, possibility, and play a meaningful part of students' intellectual experiences. Throughout the book, I try to jam, to (in the words of one reviewer) poetically provoke you, the reader, while (in the words of another) taking seriously the emotions and care that come with writing center work.

It is only in retrospect that I am able to appreciate the degree to which Todd was dis/figured by institutional failure, and I'm sure I can't fully appreciate it, even now. But since I met Todd I have experienced my own version of institutional dis/figurement. That memo was one instance. And I, like Todd, have come up against my own limitations, have tried to work within them and around them and finally through and beyond them. This book represents much of that continuing struggle. As such, it is my attempt to develop and refine and refute a philosophy of teaching and writing center work, a process that leads me to use theory to push through the limitations of my practice and to use practice to push through the limitations of my theory.[3] I hope that readers will see themselves in this project, as educators who, like me, are bumping up against the limitations of your own practices in many ways, faced with new technologies, with increasing workloads, with pressure for accountability. Educators who no longer feel at home in our homes.

For many of us, our universities are not the communities we thought they would be. Where we once imagined growing old gently languishing on green lawns, with the sun on our faces and tattered copies of [choose-your-favorite-novel-here] in our hands, we find ourselves stuffed in committee meetings, arguing with a student about a grade, or commuting from campus to campus to make endsmeat. This is not what we had in mind.

I suspect the university Todd encountered was not what he had in mind either. *The New York Times* recently carried a piece on workers in one of the local recycling plants. What a dismal job, separating recyclables from trash day after day after day. Each worker is responsible for picking out a particular type of recyclable—plastic milk jugs, for example, or juice containers, or brown glass bottles. It's easier that way. More efficient. The article ends, as we have come to expect, with the promise of the American dream: a quote from a worker who keeps this job, he says, because he has two sons whom he wants "to go to college and do something else" (Stewart 1).

As I clipped that article, I noticed a television commercial for the United Negro College Fund playing in the background. It began with a young man dressing for his first day of college. His father urges him to wear a tie: "A tie says you're serious." After a series of if-I-were-you's, the son replies, in an exasperated tone: "Dad, you're not going. *I* am." The father lowers his eyes and says softly, "I know, I know." The commercial ends with the son walking over to his dresser and retrieving a tie. The voiceover comes on: "When you're the first in your family to go, you're going for a lot of people."

I imagine sons like this to be students like Todd, arriving at college not only with their own hopes and dreams, but carrying the weight of the dreams of another generation as well, and finding within these walls not quite what they expected. Perhaps opportunities they never knew to imagine, as I found questions I would not otherwise have known to ask, but also pain. Again, maybe I've imposed this reading. But maybe not.

Dislocation is a traumatic experience, involving separation and loss even as it holds the potential for relocation and regeneration. In times of such dislocation, noise should be expected and recognized for what it is: an attempt to alert others. To warn them. To gain assistance. To garner sympathy. To raise awareness. For these reasons and more, this book asks readers to consider the kinds of noise that we are asked to make, that we are allowed to make, that we are supposed to refrain from making, as we experience dislocations in our university communities and in our professional conversations. At the same time, it encourages readers to imagine other possibilities, alternative ways of enacting a pedagogy, an administration, a profession. Imagine the noise of laughter. Of life. Of joy.

1

TUTORING AS (HARD) LABOR
The Writing Clinic, The Writing Laboratory, The Writing Center

I now direct a writing center that I *do not* imagine to be characterized by the same sense of dislocation as the one in which I worked with Todd.[1] But I can't be sure of that. In fact, I am less sure of it at this point in the semester, having just held the last class meeting of the year in my tutor-training course. The final few weeks of that course are usually marked—and this class was no exception—by a stream of students visiting my office, not to talk about end-of-term projects (as we might expect) but to work through, quietly and individually, their concerns about beginning to tutor. One after another, they express their nervousness, their uncertainty about their preparation, their concerns even about the appropriateness of their personalities. As they enter and exit my office, they parade through a writing center that, though modest in its appointments, is nonetheless bright and cheery enough, with magnetic poetry and Magna Doodles dotting its tables and student artwork on its walls. Through the doors of my office, these students can hear the low tones of talk between tutors and writers punctuated occasionally (or frequently, depending on the tutor) with bursts of laughter or with rolls of giggles. Yet they don't seem to notice. I wonder about that, and I try to remember what I felt as a beginning tutor.

I don't recall when I first realized that writing centers were called anything at all. I don't think it was when I was an undergraduate, when I rose from the table in the dining hall after lunch, announcing that I had to "go tutor." Elkins Hall was simply the place where I went to do that. I do believe, thinking back, that a faded, hand-lettered sign on the door indicated that this room housed the "Tutoring Center," but the designation seemed insignificant to me.

Such a take on tutoring seems hard to imagine now—now that I have spent more than a decade thinking about and working in writing centers, now that I am writing a book focused largely on the signification of naming, the correspondence between how we talk about ourselves (writing labs, writing clinics, writing centers) and what we do. Nevertheless, I do feel certain that the "Tutoring Center" designation *was* insignificant to me at the time. And I can't help but believe that the lack of that sign (*The Writing Center*) and my failure to identify a system within which I was working, beyond "just tutoring," were intimately related. There was no there there. I like to think, and I do have some confirmation of this, that the tutors here at Fairfield name the writing center somewhere in their job descriptions. Often I'll hear them say that they "work in the Writing Center" or that they "tutor in the Writing Center." They seem to attach a sense of place to their work, even as I become increasingly suspicious of the connection between the work of creating a community and the tutors' own experiences in the writing center. (More on this problem later in the chapter.)

This chapter, then, takes up the issue of naming not to privilege one designation over another—to assert that writing labs "experiment" on students or to claim that writing clinics "medicalize" them—but to imagine nonetheless that calling a thing a thing somehow *matters*, to consider that the ways in which we characterize work tells us something *about* that work. To do so, I will both review what others in the writing center community have written and said about the terms *clinic, lab,* and *center* as ways of imagining work with students, and I will extend those discussions in ways that I hope will prove provocative no matter what we call ourselves.

MUDDY WATERS: THE WRITING CLINIC AND
THE WRITING LAB

My initial attempts at drafting this chapter made more significant, hard-and-fast distinctions between the writing clinic and the writing laboratory, in part because considering each metaphor independently (*clinic, lab,* and *center*) seemed to be accepted practice (see Pemberton 1992 and Carino 1992) but also because, like Michael Pemberton and

Peter Carino, I had hoped to tease apart distinctions that might become fused should I consider the two in tandem.

I began by reading (and re-reading . . . and taking notes on) Foucault's *The Birth of the Clinic*, searching . . . searching . . . searching for a hook. The book was thought-provoking. It gave me lots of ideas, and they led me, ultimately, here—to a place where I have decided *not* to artificially impose distinctions between the two metaphors (*clinic* and *lab*) for which I can, frankly, find little evidence in the literature. A cop-out? We'll see.

Carino seems comfortable distinguishing between the two, arguing that the term *clinic* "degrades students by enclosing them in a metaphor of illness" (33). Quoting from the *OED*, Carino does consider the secondary sense of *clinic* as "[a]n institution, class, or conference, etc. for instruction in or the study of a particular subject; a seminar," but he ultimately rejects this notion of a writing clinic (as opposed to, say, a business clinic) because the student bodies he sees so obviously marked by visits to the writing clinic invoke, for Carino, the medicalized sense of the term.

Pemberton is more willing than Carino to see elision between the clinic metaphor and others, but he too treats it separately. The structure of his article, "The Prison, the Hospital and the Madhouse: Redefining Metaphors for the Writing Center," in fact, effectively demands that he do so, Pemberton sees the clinic as preferable to the prison and madhouse metaphors (small comfort), primarily because the clinic metaphor at least affords writing center staff a modicum of professionalism and because clinics (or hospitals, to use Pemberton's metaphor) "are places of compassion and healing" (13).

Both authors ultimately conclude that the metaphor of the clinic oversimplifies the work of the clinic and, by extension, the complexity of writing. Here's Pemberton: "Most writing problems are deeply ingrained and quite complex; they are resolved gradually, over time, often over a period of years. They do not lend themselves to quick cures or simple panaceas"(14). And Carino: "Writing clinics were associated with drill and kill pedagogy. . . . This pedagogy did not, however, consider that learning is a negotiation of new habits, values, expectations, turns of mind, strategies of representation, and the like"(34).

While Pemberton finds no redemption in metaphors other than the *center* metaphor (which I will consider later), Carino views the *lab* metaphor as providing "a powerful counter narrative, advancing a cultural ideology more akin to the ways we perceive ourselves today" (34).[2] According to Carino, labs were places where writing was more likely to be viewed as a process, where staff would be reconceiving notions of pedagogy according to this new paradigm of composition studies, where people found "a place to experiment, to pose questions, and to seek solutions" (35). Carino does admit, however, that "the metaphor of the lab came to signify a place as marginal as most clinics" (35).

That the metaphoric *lab* has more to recommend it than the metaphoric *clinic* is evidenced for Carino by the fact that the *lab* moniker persists today, despite its negative connotations, precisely because labs can also connote possibility and play (strengths of writing centers that I'd like to take up again later). As I have written elsewhere, however, writing centers have always functioned in the face of inherent contradictions, and it is a mistake, I believe, to underwrite the history of the writing center as one in which practices at any given time and among any self-identified entities are actually monolithic. (See my February 1999 *CCC* article for more on this subject.) So labs were not the only places for possibility and play. Clinics, even though their names might not have implied this, could be such places as well. In fact, one of the most progressive early centers *was* a clinic, the University of Denver's Writing Clinic, where Davidson and Sorenson, who co-directed it, advocated a psychotherapeutic approach to tutoring sessions. While psychotherapy is a medical model of sorts (and some psychotherapy did follow the diagnostic model), the tutors at the University of Denver were not drilling-and-skilling, were not diagnosing and treating, at least as far as we can tell from the published literature. They were instead advised to question and draw students out using "Rogerian nondirective counseling" (1946, 84), a precursor to the nondirective or mirroring method that dominated writing center practice for decades and is still advocated today.

We can also find a great deal of evidence in the literature of writing *labs* where drill-and-(s)kill type remediation is a priority and where cures for conditions were frequently prescribed. I am reminded of one of my favorite (so to speak) pieces of (fairly) early writing on writing labs, J.O. Bailey's "Remedial Composition for Advanced Students." Bailey, then director of the laboratory at the University of North Carolina, describes UNC's Composition Condition Laboratory (or "CC" for short), designed for students who had advanced academically but who were still poor writers (1946, 145). If an instructor thought that a student needed to work on his (or possibly her) writing, the instructor would place a "CC" behind the final grade to indicate that the student had a "composition condition" and should be sent to the lab. This lab doesn't sound like the kind of place where there were many possibilities or much play.

In fact, my readings of the early literature on writing centers convinced me that the naming of those early labs was probably largely accidental. In other words, we can tell very little—nothing reliably, really—about the work of a writing center by considering what it was called within its own institution. While many of us now spend a great deal of time inquiring as to what other centers call themselves—not only "The Writing Center" or "The Writing Lab" but "The Writer's Room" or "The Writer's Workshop"—that kind of self-conscious attention to the relationship between the signified and the signifier was absent until recently. As my earlier anecdote suggests, people in those places were, for the most part, "just tutoring." Published pieces on writing labs were quite likely to medicalize students, and published pieces on writing clinics might well report experiments on/with students. In practice, these centers were probably doing all that and more every day. And, in reality, all of our centers are probably doing all that and more still today. I know mine is.

As I played with these metaphors, as I failed to find a reliable correspondence between the name and the thing, I became more interested in the relationship *between* medicine and science, a relationship that has become increasingly less evident in our day-to-day life, where most of us deal with medical doctors who are not, or at least would not consider their primary functions to be, scientists. They are not involved in cutting-edge research; they don't work in labs; they may not even be formally affiliated with hospitals (particularly if they are primary-care physicians); and if they are affiliated with hospitals, those hospitals are likely not to be teaching hospitals or research hospitals. These people (and patient-care advocates remind us and them that they are, in fact, people) are "just" doctors. Michel Foucault makes the relationship between medicine and science seem self-evident, so the more I read, and the more I wrote, and the more I thought, the more I was forced to reconsider my original intention to distinguish between the two, *clinic* (medical) versus *lab* (scientific), in those particular terms.

I put the clinics aside for a while and turned my attention to labs, particularly to early science teaching labs. We certainly seem to take for granted in this field that writing labs were modeled on science labs, but I wanted more details. Rather than answers, I found questions. In particular, I learned that there is little agreement in the science-teaching community as to the key features of a teaching lab. Issues such as the amount of space needed for a lab (or for different types of labs) are hotly contested, funding is a constant source of distress, ideal reporting lines are debatable, course credit and full-time equivalents for graduation are confusing. It all began to sound strangely familiar.

What seemed less familiar was the gendering of the discussion. Thirteen of the fifteen articles to which I was referred had been authored by men; discussions on the National Association for Research in Science Teaching (NARST) listserv to which I subscribed were dominated by male voices. What was I to make of the nagging feeling I got from these NARST threads? It took an exchange between two students to prompt me.

Martin, the one male student who shows up at our end of the semester meeting for potential tutors, sits quietly in his seat as I talk about procedures and policies in the Writing Center: *This is how students sign up for appointments in the Writing Center. This is the database into which records need to be inputted. This is the schedule you will fill out to tell me your preferred hours. Blah, blah, blah, blah.*

Any questions?

A few students have questions of clarification. And finally, a soft "okay" from Martin's side of the room as his hand lifts halfway. I acknowledge him, and he asks with a smirk, "Uh . . . Am I going to be the only *guy* tutoring in the Writing Center?"

I offer a "Probably" followed by a quick "but": "But we've had male tutors in the past; we just happen not to have any right now." True enough. But. When we *have* had male tutors, they have been in the extreme minority—one, at most two or (during really wild times) three, out of a staff of approximately twelve.

One woman asks Martin if he has "a problem with that," to which he dutifully replies, "No." Another student then asks why this is and whether our situation is typical. This is not the discussion I had planned. (They so rarely are, aren't they?)

I am apt to forget (until I am reminded, until I am on a listserv for scientists, until a student asks a question about the male-female ratio/n in the writing center) the extent to which I am engaged in work that is historically feminized. Even once I am reminded, I have to think hard, over and over again, about what this means.

The feminization of composition studies—and particularly of composition teaching (of which writing centers are obviously one manifestation)—remains an issue that has been subjected to a fair amount of analysis. In *Textual Carnivals: The Politics of Composition,* Susan Miller (1991) distinguishes between a gendered division of the labor of composition and a sexual division of that labor. Miller argues that a gendered reading highlights the degree to which these activities express social power relations rather than mere (or exclusively) biological distinctions. In a chapter entitled "The Sad Women in the Basement," Miller nods to Freudian psychoanalysis to consider the "matrix of functions" (136) working to feminize the composition instructor:

> [O]ne figure of a composition teacher is overloaded with symbolic as well as actual functions. These functions include the dual (or even triple)

roles that are washed together in these teachers: the nurse who cares for and tempts her young charge toward "adult" uses of language that will not "count" because they are, for now, engaged in only with hired help; the "mother" (tongue) that is an ideal/idol and can humiliate, regulate, and suppress the child's desires; and finally the disciplinarian, now not a father figure but a sadomasochistic Barbarella version of either maid or mother. (137)

Miller herself notes the irony of this fledgling professional field of study invoking the scientific model of paradigms in a desperate attempt to legitimize work that is otherwise feminized in every major aspect of its analysis: socially, culturally, economically. She writes,

The juxtaposition of these terms [*process paradigm*] does not, I would argue, unconsciously preserve androgyny and thereby give equal privileges to two terms of a pair that is symbolically female and male, yin and yang. Instead, the choice of this seemingly contradictory pair in a new description of composition teaching and theory contains two equal preservations of the historical (traditional, hegemonic) situation of composition. *Process* practices extend and preserve literary subjectivity, while their explanation in a *paradigm* theory extends and preserves the anxiety about status that has always been associated with English studies, both in regard to the perfection of elitist texts and as a professional concern about identity in relation to older, "harder" disciplines. (140)[3]

In the end, we are left with a topsy-turvy rendering of scientized sites like *clinics* and *laboratories* full of *women* doing the *laboring*.

Labor. Perhaps first and foremost the word assumes the connotation of "man's work" (as in *hard labor*), calls up images of men bent over building materials or microscopes. But it is of course multi-accented, carrying with it Marxist notions of a laboring underclass of proletariat workers and notions of re/production (specifically *female* reproduction). In particular, it could lead us to consider the ways that women's work—the cleaning up of the grammar, the kiss-the-red-ink-and-make-it-better—is defined within a framework that is structured by men (the clinic, the lab) and that frees men to do the "real work": engage with interesting ideas, mentor the "smart" students, do their own writing.

I want to commandeer this discussion of labs and clinics, wrest it away from the associations under which it has been laboring. Let it *breathe-breathe-breathe.*

LAMAZE, LABOR, AND THE TAYLORIZATION OF THE WRITING CENTER

Nearly a decade ago, Donna Haraway referred to Richard Gordon's use of the term "homework economy" to describe

> . . . a restructuring of work that broadly has the characteristics formerly ascribed to female jobs, jobs literally done only by women. Work is being redefined as both literally female and feminized, whether performed by men or women. To be feminized means to be made extremely vulnerable; able to be disassembled, reassembled, exploited as a reserve labour force; seen less as workers than as servers; subjected to time arrangements on and off the paid job that make a mockery of a limited work day; leading an existence that always borders on being obscene, out of place, and reducible to sex. (1991, 166)

More recently, in a *Harper's* article entitled "Maid to Order: The Politics of Other Women's Work," Barbera Ehrenreich considers the implications of the growing middle-class reliance on household services. Ehrenreich observes, "[I]n a society in which 40 percent of the wealth is owned by 1 percent of households while the bottom 20 percent reports negative assets, the degradation of others is readily purchased" (2000, 59). I thought of Ehrenreich last night as I knelt bent over shelves in our new (a relative term, to be sure) house, scoring and sponging and scouring shelf paper from the insides of drawers and closets and cabinets, to ready them for the painter (whom we've hired) and for the "tile guy" (whom we've also hired). I wondered, while I was working, whether there wasn't also someone/anyone whom we could hire to do what I was doing: the dirty work. "We can afford it, can't we?" I wondered aloud to my husband.

I was happy to get back to writing this morning, in my air-conditioned office, where all the light switches work and where there's no damp, musty smell of a closed-up house mixed with cannabis and cat piss. It wasn't so hard to scoooot my chair in and start to *typ-typ-typ-type* here in the Ivory Tower.

"[T]he cleaning lady," according to Ehrenreich, is positioned (quite literally) "as *dea ex machina*, restoring tranquillity as well as order to the home. Marriage counselors recommend her as an alternative to squabbling, as do many within the cleaning industry itself" (62). If in the 1960s and 1970s housecleaning was primarily a question of gender—wives were expected to clean inside the home and husbands were expected to work outside of it—Ehrenreich argues that now "the politics of housework is becoming a politics not only of gender but of race and class—and these are subjects that . . . most Americans generally prefer to avoid" (63).

Academic cleaning services, like writing centers, house their share of the politics of race, gender, and class. Like the general American public, our institutions also prefer to avoid these discussions (unless, of course, the discussions *celebrate* the *diversity* of our institutions of higher learning). Even those of us who work in writing centers, those of us who are quick to assign blame to our institutions for their failures, are loath to turn a critical eye on ourselves and on the role our own writing centers might play in further entrenching a have/have-not economy of the university.[4]

The proliferation of cleaning services has resulted in what Ehrenreich calls an "intense Taylorization" that "makes the work . . . factorylike," more (for the purposes of our later discussion) efficient (66).[5] She describes, for example, the strict order in which rooms in homes were to be cleaned: "Deviation was subject to rebuke, as I found when I was caught moving my arm from right to left while wiping Windex over a French door" (66). Pedagogical requirements can lend a factory-like air to the writing center sessions of even the most well-meaning tutor, as she works with the eighteenth paper from the same Info Systems class or anticipates the fanatical grammatical critique of a professor with whom she herself has struggled. Though I try to shield the tutors from rebuke (other than those they visit upon themselves, over which I have little control), they know that they are likely to be perceived as deviating from the norm by their mere presence.

Several years ago, two tutors reluctantly pointed an irate faculty member in the direction of my office. When I greeted him with a how-are-you, he replied that he was very upset, thank you, as he had sent an ESL student to the writing center to work on a draft and her paper, when it was returned to him, was still *dirty*, filled with inappropriate usage and grammatical mistakes. I explained to him how we work with ESL students and reminded him (as he surely already knew, given his area of expertise) that acquiring a second language is a slow, developmental process. I then suggested that, had the tutor simply *corrected* all the mistakes, this same professor would likely be in my office blessing me out because the tutor had done *too much work* for the student. He admitted that this was probably true.

The tutors, for their part, have difficulty maintaining the strict boundary that constitutes a student's *own* work when students so frequently arrive with papers filled with the *professor's* comments, with ideas about the paper the *professor* wanted to see written, with evidence that the *professor* feels justified in having little regard for these same boundaries. Just last week, a student arrived, introducing her dilemma using an impressive array of expletives, with an outline penned by her professor on the back of her draft. The professor introduced the outline to the student by stating simply, "These are your ideas." They were, of course, not the student's ideas.

In the conclusion to her essay, Ehrenreich issues a "moral challenge . . . to make work visible again: not only the scrubbing and vacuuming but all the hoeing, stacking, hammering, drilling, bending, and lifting that goes into creating and maintaining a livable habitat" (70). The scrubbing and hoeing and tending that went on in the aforementioned session was admirable. Kristen, the tutor, took a student who came in sullen—with the attitude that she was "transferring anyway"—and painstakingly, methodically, figured out where the professor had gone wrong. The session began by focusing on the professor's repeated remarks that the paper, as it stood, employed "circular reasoning." The student didn't understand what that meant. Kristen suspected that the professor's outline might suggest a way to sequence the argument more logically. Upon studying the outline, however, Kristen realized that the teacher had misunderstood the student's point and had created an outline that in fact misrepresented the student's argument. The student seemed to want to try to work off of the outline, even though she neither agreed with it nor understood it. So Kristen had a new task: she suggested that they put the professor's outline aside and just do their own outline. They did. The session was punctuated by moments where Kristen instructed the student not only on writing, but also on intellectual integrity. "Sometimes you have to go with what the teacher wants," Kristen said at one point, "But this isn't going to be *her* paper. Sometimes you just need to disregard what a prof says."

Needless to say, Kristen was distressed after the session. I tried, as I often do, to offer both the sinister and the benign interpretations of the professor's outline. She may have had, I suggested, five students lined up outside her door waiting to see her. Kristen acknowledged that possibility, but she concluded our meeting with the following thought: "You know what really bothers me? Making that outline is more than just making that outline, you know? There's something behind that." Yeah. I know.

I can see why the writing center becomes the hard-labor camp of the academy. What would happen if we were to seize that designation, admit that the writing center is indeed a place where actual labor (*gasp!*) takes place, look our colleagues in the eyes and say, yes, we work with our hands. We take texts and we turn them around and over and upside down; we cut them into their bits and pieces; we tug at them, tutor to student, student to tutor, back and forth, to and fro, tug-tug-tug. We ball up ideas and we pitch them, sometimes to each other, sometimes away—*three points!*—into the trash. (Omygodcanwedothat?!)

Setting metaphors in motion appeals to me. It gets me thinking less about the structural entities themselves as foundational—*the* lab, *the* clinic, *the* center—and more about the fundamental moments being played out *in* them, shifting the terms of the discussion "by leaping out of a 'mechanics of solids' and into a discussion of *fluidity*" (Davis 2000, 166, quoting Irigaray). Davis again offers a framework for loosening these metaphors when she observes, "Fluids are leaky; they do not stay put; they cannot be fixed in an appropriation" (166).

There's no escaping fluids and leaks in discussions of labor—childbirth and labor, that is. Breasts leak; water breaks. A pregnant woman's body exceeds its own boundaries (so much so that complete strangers often think nothing of reaching out to touch a protruding belly). Yet the only metaphor that comes close to approaching the labor-and-delivery model of writing center work—the midwife metaphor—presents a sanitized, romanticized version of the goings-on. This metaphor is routinely championed for its gentleness, its sensitivity, its attention to process. In her article "Giving Birth to Voice: The Professional Writing Tutor as Midwife," Donna Rabuck frames the difference this way:

> In contrast to doctors within the medical hierarchy who tend to view birth as a product, an isolated event that results in a child, midwives view birth as a normal, healthy process not dependent on heavy intervention or extreme mechanical manipulation. While most doctors see pregnant women for brief periods of time and rely on scientific information to chart their progress, midwives tend to devote more time to talking with pregnant women, asking and answering questions that have to do with mental as well as physical health, finding out what their clients need to know, and providing information in language they can understand. (1995, 113)

When Rabuck extends this glorious role of the midwife to the tutoring context, I object, as I read, to every single assumption she makes: the idea that sessions (or births) proceed gently and smoothly (113); the positioning of the midwife/tutor as a "translator [of] expectations" (114); the Cassandra-like persecution complex of the eternally marginalized and misunderstood (117). Enough.

Where is the noise?!

While I have no doubt that there are genuine benefits to having a midwife attend to a woman's pregnancy and childbirth and while I certainly agree that pregnancy and childbirth are natural-enough phenomena (for some women), I wonder why we insist on framing it as a zen-like experience, and I certainly wonder why that zen-like characterization is the one that gets foisted upon the midwife tutor. Are we afraid that no one will do it if we talk about the real deal? The bloody plug, the protruding veins, the vomiting, the potential complications. The screams of pain; the tears of joy (or, sometimes, the wails of sorrow). Do we think people won't be willing to take that risk?

Where *is the noise?!*

In an article chronicling the evolution of sound and cinematography, Walter Murch, writing in *The New York Times*, has this to say about the primacy of sound during fetal development:

> [F]our and a half months after we are conceived, we are already beginning to hear. It is the first of our senses to be switched on, and for the next four and a half months sound reigns as a solitary Queen of the Senses. The close and liquid world of the womb makes sight and smell impossible, taste and touch a dim and generalized hint of what is to come. Instead, we luxuriate in a continuous bath of sounds: the song of our mother's voice, the swash of her breathing, the piping of her intestines, the timpani of her heart. (2000, 1)

And then, I would add, when it all comes so abruptly to a halt, the first thing a healthy baby does is let out a great, big *holler!*

I went to visit a friend in the hospital after she had just given birth (with the help of a midwife) to her second child, a baby boy. We talked, as you might expect, about the labor and delivery, and she summed it up, with great intensity, this way: "It was sooooo painful, but it was sooooo worth it."

KEEP OUT OF THIS HOUSE: ILL-LITERACY, A COMMUNICABLE DISEASE[6]

It became a running joke in class last semester that our discussions of tutoring always ended with my admission that the job is "impossible." Frankly, I think it is. Tutors are placed, on a daily basis, in impossible positions. Despite this, students flock to the tutoring class and then to the Writing Center because that im/possibility is the challenge, is the passion. First-generation tutors beget second-generation tutors by convincing a roommate or a fellow major or a compadre from some other common campus organization to take the class, give it a try. Tutoring is *sooooo painful*. But it's *sooooo worth it*. In fact, we might even say it's *infectious*.

Of course, we lament, however, that it is not. If tutoring were infectious, we might argue, writing center work would have revolutionized the teaching of writing by now, sixteen years after Stephen North (1984) first articulated the discontent of so many writing center staff in this regard. If tutoring were infectious, we wouldn't still see "Go to the writing center!" penned at the end of an essay. Writing centers wouldn't still be tied to remediation, both physically (in many cases) and psychologically (in most cases). We wouldn't still be running on soft money, in soft positions, in soft spaces. Unless we were quarantined.

I admit that I sometimes feel that the tutors and I have been quarantined. Judging from the litany of complaints in the literature and on the writing center listserv about people's basement spaces, about their tangential relationships to university life and resources, I would say that others might agree. So how about a self-imposed quarantine? An admission to our university communities that we too, like our students, are infected?

Referring to the type of writing usually taught in composition classrooms, Davis quotes Avital Ronnell who calls the work "hygienic writing" and the "self-cleaning text" (2000, 99). Ronnell writes, "Each thinking text, to the extent that it develops strategies of protection against outside interference or parasitism, is run by an immunological drive" (99). Students strive to produce antibacterial texts, impervious to the germ of an idea that might be subject to critique. Their writing is driven by the anticipation of problems. Yet their allegedly germ-free texts result in resistant strains of commentary, and even such sanitized texts as our students routinely produce are deemed *unwashed*. This is how a colleague winds up at my door with questions about an ESL student's paper. This is how a student winds up in the writing center with the outline of a paper that she can't begin to write. This is how "we [academics/philosophers of language] are called into the vocations of cleanup crew for the sanitation department of the philosophical enterprise." Still, "even the most effective cleanup crew isn't perfect. Even after a text has been sanitized, the most suspicious of snoots will detect a lingering odor. Interestingly enough, the cleanup crew itself, which necessarily, as Ronell notes, 'retains traces of [the] filth' it is hired to purify, becomes infected and so is *infectious*" (Davis 100).

The notion that we are infected, that our students have somehow infected us and infect each other, will no doubt strike some as odd, as irresponsible, perhaps even as sheer blasphemy.[7] Absolutely. But don't we all sometimes . . . come on . . . admit it . . . feel dis/eased? What about at lunch, at a table full of colleagues, when we're listening for the umpteenth time to one or another's diatribe on the Decline of Standards, on the Death of Literacy? Or at a committee meeting on (water) Retention? (Administrative) Bloat? On OutComes-(urp)-Assessment? Don't we all feel just a little . . . *sick?*

Such ill-health is not surprising given that our universities— that *we*—may be more interested in the cleanly *appearance* of student texts than in the genuine condition of the texts and the ideas they re/present. Returning to Ehrenreich's "Maid to Order," we learn that Taylorized, efficiency-driven operations are, ironically, "not very sanitary" (2000, 67). Ehrenreich, for her part, concludes, "The point is not so much to clean as to appear to have cleaned, not to sanitize but to create a kind of stage setting for family life" (67). The point is, perhaps, at least as Kristen's student initially understood it, not to straighten out the logic in your own argument but to mis/represent the argument the professor has erroneously assigned to you.

A self-imposed quarantine, then, might mean that we would have to admit that we, like our students, are neither clean nor particularly sanitary. And, worse yet, that there is no such thing, really, as a quarantine since we would still have to be worried, as Davis notes, about the *lllleaksss*. About the noise seeping through the cracks, around the door jam, down the hall. About the students who would continue to arrive at our doors hoping to "get clean," looking for, as Michael Blitz and Mark Hurlbert have written, "a weekly 'fix'—a jolt of correctives to their works" (2000, 88).

Post-anythings (-modernism, -structuralism, -disciplinarity) leave the integrity of the subject in crisis. They take an entity that we assumed to be a w/hole, a unit, a self-contained, intact being and they expose the cracks in its foundation(alism). Labs-and-clinics/science-and-medicine in the late-twentieth/early-twenty-first century meet with the disintegration and re-configuration of the body. Baboon hearts have given way to heart-lung transplants to skin grafts and cloning. In the face of such mind-boggling developments, it stands to reason that we are forced to find new ways of conceptualizing the w/hole, of thinking about the fragmentation of the self. Post-any-things teach me that closing the door may create a boundary of a sort, may provide a defense mechanism against future complaints ("Well, we closed the door!") but that doing so offers a false measure of security, and a costly one at that, involving a loss of potential(ities). The boundary is permeable, with the noise, as I know from my own approaches to the Writing Center, still traveling up and down the hall. The closed door signals an unwillingness to engage, a refusal to ask *What is it I hear that others fail to hear?* How is it that these tones remain undifferentiated for PC (of the Prologue), that he can be so completely dismissive of them, characterizing them as "such a racket" and wishing for a little "peace and quiet"? Why am I suddenly trans-ported out of my office and into another hallway, the hallway of our family home, a thousand miles and twenty years away, where we walked on eggshells and tiptoes during my grandfather's nap time, so as not to provoke his "[deep] disappoint[ment]" and paternalistic diatribes on "appropriate[ness]"(PC)?

THE CENTER CAN/NOT (w)HOL(e)D

Here is a kind of question, let us still call it historical, whose conception, formation, gestation, and labor we are only catching a glimpse of today. I employ these words, I admit, with a glance toward the operations of childbearing— but also with a glance toward those who, in a society from which I do not exclude myself, turn their eyes away when faced by the as yet unnamable which is proclaiming itself and which can do so, as is necessary whenever a birth is in the offing, only under the species of the nonspecies, in the formless, mute, infant, and terrifying form of monstrosity. (Derrida 1978, 293)

In a sense, the cyborg has no origin story in the Western sense—a "final" irony since the cyborg is also the awful apocalyptic telos of the "West's" escalating dominations of abstract individuation, an ultimate self untied at last from all dependency, a man in space. An origin story in the "Western," humanist sense depends on the myth of original unity, fullness, bliss and terror, represented by the phallic mother from whom all humans must separate, the task of individual development and of history . . . The main trouble with cyborgs, of course, is that they are the illegitimate offspring of militarism and patriarchal capitalism, not to mention state socialism. But illegitimate offspring are often exceedingly unfaithful to their origins. Their fathers, after all, are inessential. (Haraway1991, 150-151)

In "Structure, Sign and Play," Jacques Derrida offers "two interpretations of interpretation," two ways of imagining the mythology of the myth, the history of the history: "The one seeks to decipher . . . a truth or an origin which escapes play and the order of the sign. . . . The other, which is no longer turned toward the origin, affirms play and tries to pass beyond man and humanism, [beyond the dream] of full presence, the reassuring foundation, the origin and the end of play" (292). As author, I see my own book in both of Derrida's interpretations: as a project now working against the certainty of the w/hole, the centeredness of the (writing) center, yet as a project beginning seven years ago with dissertation research and a drive to uncover the historical *origins* of writing centers, their "true" practice, in colleges and universities. In my sessions with Todd, in my work with tutors, in my classroom encounters with students, in my research and writing, I did not find, I do not find, what I expected and expect to find. What I continue to find, however, is always much more play-full than I ever anticipated.

A search for the birth of the writing lab/clinic/center would take us back, but to where? To the admission of the *unwashed* to prestigious universities like Harvard in the late nineteenth century (Miller 1991; Berlin 1987)? To the conferencing method of the 1880s (Lerner)? To self-sponsored writing groups (Gere 1987)? To open admissions? To the start of *The Writing Lab Newsletter* and *The Writing Center Journal* (1978 and 1980, respectively)? Yes. Yes. Yes. To all of them. Our search should take us back to these places and more and more and more and more: To the "numberless beginnings whose faint traces and hints of color are readily seen by an historical eye" (Foucault 1995, 145). This is how we can begin to tell the histories of the histories of our writing centers, to become writing center genealogists, in the Foucauldian sense of the term.

By the time I began my path of composition teaching and research, *writing center* was the naturalized term for this place where tutors and writers sat and worked on pieces of writing. Indeed, this is the reason I have selected it as the default term even when talking about published pieces on labs and clinics. With the notable exception of the Purdue Writing Lab (and the attendant *Writing Lab Newsletter*, both of which are overseen by Muriel Harris), the terms *lab* and *clinic* are used specifically to invoke a *past* moment in the histories of our writing centers. Our regional organizations, our national organization, our refereed journal, our listserv—all make specific references to the *centeredness* of our undertaking. This is not, however, to say that the idea of a *center* occupies uncontested space. Quite the contrary.

While no one is seriously trying to rescue the lab/clinic titles (at least not in print), the center terminology is championed periodically for its appropriateness in describing how we might want to be viewed by our institutions. Carino, for example, offers a definition of *center* that "evokes the communal aspect of the center as a microculture in which camaraderie replaces the competitive atmosphere of the classroom" (1992, 38). Another sense of the term, he adds, offers us "a bold and audacious metaphor aspiring to powerful definitions as in 'the center of a circle, of revolution, of centripetal attraction; and connected uses'" (38). He does warn, however, that this sense "carries the dangers of assimilation as well as the potential for empowerment as it further imbricates writing centers in university culture, *defining them beyond the nurturing communities they often see themselves as*" (38, emphasis added).

In that same issue of *The Writing Center Journal*, Richard Leahy publishes an article that considers specifically and only the notion of the center for writing centers, focusing on two of the word's forms—*centeredness* and *centrism*—the former having more positive connotations for Leahy than the latter. Leahy offers a personal definition of centeredness that revolves around "a sense of purpose and community, of knowing 'who you are'" (1992, 43), a sense he deems especially important as writing centers grow larger and take on additional cross-curricular responsibilities. Much of Leahy's article takes up the potential threats to community in the writing center, drawn from his own personal experience: specifically, a staff that gets too large or becomes too professional and the tenure-track status of the director (which drew him away from the center for committee work and for a sabbatical, resulting in a team of tutors not selected by him). As he traces these problems, Leahy refers repeatedly to things that "[work] against community" (44), to the need for a "feeling of family and teamwork" (45), to community as "purpose" as "mission" (46). Community, community, community. Hold on a minute there . . . You're *b-b-b-r-r-e-a-k-i-n-g u p!*

I don't necessarily disagree that the items Leahy singles out can present challenges, even problems, if we want to call them that. A large staff, a professionalized staff, committee work, a sabbatical—all have resulted at one time or another in critical unease in my writing center as well. So I'm not sure why I reacted so strongly to Leahy's continual reassertion of a writing center community.[8] In truth, it may be because, after seven years of directing a writing center, I have grown tired of re-creating community in the writing center year after year after year (and it's only been seven!), most often to see my offspring become unfaithful to me. And I've begun to ask myself if maybe, quite possibly, *I* am the problem. Not for the reasons Leahy cites, though, as I said, I am guilty of all of the things he mentions. I am a problem for other reasons: for trying to "organize" the beginning of the year gathering, for "setting up" the holiday party, for ensuring that there's always food around (which the tutors of course appreciate). For imagining that these efforts might *create* a sense of community rather than *emerge from* one.

For hosting a holiday party to which no one came, even though they promised. They promised.

Leahy's *community* takes on the cloak of ontology, as though saying it makes it so: "Having completed all the requirements for a degree in community, I now confer upon you—*ta-daaah*—a degree in community." But it's not so.

Davis considers the underpinnings of feminist pedagogies designed to foster a sense of community among participants.[9] She writes,

> Feminist pedagogy itself, Nancy Schniedewind suggests, is about encouraging the "feminist values of community, communication, equality, and mutual nurturance" (171). Schniedewind even suggests that such an atmosphere might be promoted, in part, by building "festive procedures" into the run of the course. "Festive procedures," she says, "are community builders. Refreshments during breaks of long classes, a potluck dinner on occasion, and the integration of poetry and songs into the course, all catalyze energy and build solidarity" (172). (Davis 2000, 214)

Critiquing this position, Davis argues that "the pedagogue in such a course performs the role of the social lubricant, the instigator of 'participatory decision-making' and 'cooperative goal-structuring' (173-74)" (Davis 214).

When students resist our attempts to create a community in the writing center, we should ask ourselves what to make of their repeated and systematic denials. I've decided that the fact that former tutors keep me updated on personal and professional milestones, stop in for lunch when they're passing through town, or arrange for us to meet in New York for dinner and a museum or two does *not* mean that there was some communal writing center experience for which they are nostalgic. It does not necessarily mean that I created a writing center community from which they benefitted. I've finally decided that such a community is not mine to create; it is not mine to sustain.

Lil Brannon and Stephen North comment on this problem in a recent issue of *The Writing Center Journal*, acknowledging that "[o]ne of the strengths of the writing center is also a clear weakness" (2000,

11). They write, "The writing center is able to stay exciting and fresh because yearly it is always remaking itself. Yet the problems of remaking are many" (11).

Interestingly, it was North who, along with Kenneth Bruffee, ushered in the concept of a writing center community. I am pinpointing 1984 as a pivotal year in writing center history in this respect, with the publication in quick succession of both Bruffee's "Peer Tutoring and the 'Conversation of Mankind'" and North's "The Idea of a Writing Center." Though the tones of the two pieces differ dramatically, both authors articulate a model of writing center practice that depends (if only implicitly) upon community and speculate on that model's implication for the university at large. Bruffee begins his piece by chronicling the shift he has seen in his own writing center since moving from faculty tutors to peer tutors, a movement that "made learning a two-way street, since students' work tended to improve when they got help from peer tutors and tutors learned from the students they helped and from the activity of tutoring itself" (1984, 4). In this regard, according to Bruffee, peer tutoring "did not seem to change what people learned but, rather, the social context in which they learned it" (4). Bruffee relies on this idea of *social context* throughout the essay, linking it to conversation, to "a writers' community of readers and other writers" (8) and to, on more than one occasion, "a community of knowledgeable peers" (8). Peers work together in a given community, Bruffee explains, to experience learning as "an activity in which people work collaboratively to create knowledge among themselves by socially justifying belief" (12).

There would seem to be little doubt that the social nature of writing centers changed when they became staffed primarily by peers rather than by faculty. Savvy writing center directors have highlighted this change, both in philosophical terms (as Bruffee's article demonstrates) and in physical terms, describing the character of their writing centers (couches, plants, and coffee pots are *de rigueur*) in terms that differentiate the centers from the sterile classroom experiences of most college students. Community would flow naturally from these new, more social settings, the literature would have us believe, and the nature of the writing centers, where small groups of people often work together quite closely for several years, seems well suited to community formation. Certainly most writing centers hope to present faces that appear welcoming to outsiders (like us?) and to students who may feel left out of the general university community. To turn the tables on the university quarantine and self-impose it instead.

From North's initial (1984) line, "[t]his is an essay that began out of frustration," readers must be prepared for an argument from North that is much more strident than Bruffee's in its insistence that there is an *us* in this community (though North never uses this word) pitted against a *them*. While conflict is largely absent in Bruffee's piece—Bruffee never even alludes to, for example, what must have been considerable difficulties in gaining faculty support for peers to replace faculty tutors—conflict is actually a galvanizing force in North's piece. "Idea of a Writing Center" is replete with examples of the ways in which goals of the writing center staff often fly in the face of institutional goals (as those goals are represented by faculty, by administrators, even by the students themselves). North offers a decidedly Woolfian interpretation of the value of the writing center, one emphasizing the necessity of room and time and teachable moments. "Idea" has been canonized, then, not only for what it says about the *methods* of writing center staff (although North himself has reconsidered some aspects of this philosophy [in North 1994]) but also for what it suggests about the writing center's community of professionalized practitioners.

By the time Bruffee and North published these pieces, a discernible movement was afoot in writing centers: regional associations had begun to organize, *The Writing Lab Newletter* and *The Writing Center Journal* were establishing solid circulations. Previously isolated writing center staff members could plug into a growing national network of common successes and travails. The International Writing Centers Association (IWCA), *The Writing Center Journal, The Writing Lab Newsletter*, the *Wcenter* listserv—all share the same basic presumption of members of many communities or organizations: that people with common concerns benefit from sharing those experiences with their peers. I have certainly been the beneficiary of the good will of my writing center colleagues, and I hope that I have bestowed good will on my peers in turn. Nevertheless, I have been puzzled over the years by the continual reassertion of community in those regional and national writing center forums as I have learned that we can agree on virtually *no* characteristics that could identify us as a community—not a name, not status for directors, not status of staff, not practice. The list goes on. In fact, IWCA efforts at developing an accrediting arm have been thwarted (and rightly so, I believe) in part by our inability to articulate fundamental agreed-upon tenets of administration and practices such as those I've listed above (among others). In light of our agreement to disagree on virtually every aspect of our operations (short of the fact that we do all provide some sort of tutoring in writing), shouldn't we be wondering, What is this thing we're calling a writing center *community?*

Perhaps I stand accused right now in some readers' minds of being exceedingly unfaithful to my origins—to those members of the writing center community who have welcomed me over the years. Heretic. It makes me nervous, but I press on because I feel like I want to *p-u-s-h!* (Breathe-breathe-breathe.)

Davis helps me think differently about community when she writes, "The 'essence' of community/communication in a posthumanist world is the exposition of finitude and *not a bond*, which is always already *bondage*, always already at work silencing the difference of our finitude—the very thing that makes community possible" (2000, 193). Like Bruffee, like Leahy, like even North, Davis is concerned with what members of a community *share*, but that thing-that-is-what's-shared, according to Davis, "is the exposition of finite being, the exposure of an in-common (but unsharable) mortality and singularity that are not communicable but that are irrepressibly exposed/shared" (192).

I read these quotes for the first time as I tallied up the final grades for my tutoring and writing course, and I panicked: Have I prepared the tutors to have a moment like this with another person? And if I haven't, what *have* I done? But if I *have,* what have I done?! How much easier to teach them to outline a draft, to identify and refine a thesis statement, to correct errant commas.

So Davis urges us to believe in community but . . . "[r]esist imagining this community as 'communion,' as fusion, as the kind of melting together exemplified by *Star Trek*'s Vulcan mind-meld. Communion names the final culmination of sharing, the *end* of sharing—it is a desire for closure, for finality . . . [W]hat community shares is not the 'annulment of sharing;' what it shares is *sharing itself*" (194).

A conversation overheard by a tutor in the residence hall lounge:
Student 1: I went to the Writing Center with my paper today.
Student 2: What was that like?
Student 1: Well, we just kinda talked. [Long pause.] I think it helped.

Haraway's remark about illegitimate offspring helps me make sense of one set of competing narratives (the one that locates the original im/pulse for writing centers in administrative concerns about the appropriateness of student bodies, doing battle with the one that writes the writing center as somehow managing to exceed that original im/pulse, to morph into something . . . Other). Davis's definition of community—"what it shares is *sharing* itself"—also quiets some of the noise in my own head (not, mind you, that this is always desirable, but sometimes it is necessary). Taken together, Haraway's and Davis's points illustrate the appeal of community to a set of (writing center) workers whose specific charge (literacy education) appears central to institutional work but whose presence is often quite marginal. This central/marginal debate is a longstanding one in writing center literature. Offered as evidence of centrality might be a writing center's cross-curricular impact, the built-in budget, the director's permanent status. Just as often, a writing center's rescued furnishings, its basement location, its soft money and frequent turnover may be taken as proof of its marginality. Ultimately,

I'll admit, marginality is more romantic—it's more "radical"—even as it, like community, results in a familiar writing center paradox: the center's anti-disciplinary appeal is precisely its difficulty; its fluidity directly challenges its sustainability; its anti-foundationalism flies in the face of the static nature of *the* margin and *the* center.

Rather than adhering to the marginal mindset that writing center staff are "underdogs" (a mindset perceived by Harris and Kinkead 8), "renegades, outsiders, boundary dwellers, subversive" (K. Davis 8), rather than assuming that writing centers arise *from* the margins, exist *on* the margins, and are populated *by* the marginal, we might instead view writing center staff and students as *bastardizing* the work of the institution. That is, we might say that they are not a threat from *without* but are rather a threat from *within*. We might seize the designation of institutional illegitimacy as a way of explaining our lack of faithfulness to our origins. (*Their fathers, after all, are inessential.*) Haraway offers the example of the regenerative potential of the salamander that loses a limb (1991, 181). Though the salamander can grow another one, we can't be sure, really, what that limb is going to look like. It certainly won't be a perfect replica of the old one. And it could even turn out to be Monstrous.

Such a monstrosity exceeds expectations for the "normal" and that excess, for those of us who work in writing centers, is potentially a way in/out/around the central/marginal/community quagmire we've been stuck in for too long. The question of whether our practices are central to the work of our universities is closely aligned with the degree to which those practices adhere to institutional expectations. The degree of our marginality, in contrast, corresponds to the extent to which we fail to adhere to those expectations (and to the extent to which our institutions fail us). What PC witnessed in our writing center that October evening were not practices that in any way appeared central to him, though they were certainly central to us. This, he (and others) may view as a failure on our part. The centrality of the practices he encountered—the laughter, the food, the lack of a well-defined hierarchy—may indeed contribute to the writing center's marginality. If so, then our institutions are certainly failing us.

Not long ago, I requested PC's permission to use his original memo in this book. I appeared in his office and told him that I wasn't sure whether he knew that I had been working on a book and that the book was in fact entitled *Noise from the Writing Center.* A flash of recognition crossed his face as he laughed, a bit embarrassed. I thanked him for this great gift, this wonderful research direction. He graciously granted permission for use of the memo, though not before re-reading it, along with my response to it. In the end, he said that he still agreed with his memo's original premise, and he asked me what I thought about mine. I said I still agreed with my memo, too. We laughed and sat talking about our summer research projects for the better part of an hour.

I have a hard time, after a meeting like this one with PC, four years down the road, believing still that this project is doomed. I am inclined to believe instead that our writing centers grow out of institutions that continually outgrow themselves. And we have to hope for some monstrosities along the way. Maybe even tweak the helix a bit here and there to ensure them.

2

CHANNELING JIMI HENDRIX
or Ghosts in the Feedback Machine

Ear always came after eye in the creative process.
Trinh Minh-Ha, on learning the importance
of the soundtrack to film production. (202)

On June 28, 2000, the Arts and Entertainment section of *The New York Times* covered the opening of Seattle's Experience Music Project (Hendrix fans will recognize the reference in the project's title), focusing particularly on the museum's showpiece, a work entitled *If 6 Was 9* (also known as *Roots and Branches*), "a giant sound sculpture made up of 600 guitars strung along the branches of a metal tree rising more than 30 feet into the air," and on the sculptor of the piece, Trimpin (like Cher and Madonna—one name only, please). The article chronicles Trimpin's "more-than-20-year obsession with turning acoustic instruments into sculptures that can be played by motors or by valves that release water, air and even fire." Particular attention is given to prototypes of *If 6 Was 9*, a dozen or so "player" guitars strung along the walls, set in motion by striking a key on Trimpin's computer.

Trimpin traces his interest in such experimental instrumentation to his childhood. His fire organ, for example, ("a thermodynamic organ that uses a glass flame in a Pyrex tube to produce sound") harkens back to the bonfires he used to go to as a child. There, residents of the town would heat wooden discs in the fire and launch them into the air. Trimpin recalls that, while others watched the glowing objects being hurled into the distance, he was (*shhhhhh*) listening: "I could always hear choirs singing and whole symphony orchestras playing in the sounds created by this tremendous heat. . . . I always looked forward to going to the bonfire because I could listen to this symphony" (Strauss 2000, A5).

By the end of the article, Trimpin is readying himself for a James Brown concert that evening. His parting comment? "I like to go to concerts and galleries and museums, but when I go to the junkyard I have the same experience, because I can fantasize about discovering things. So junkyards and museums and concerts are all on the same level for me: there are inspirations to be found at all of them" (A5).

I start with Trimpin simply because this piece is so appealing to me. I want to give it to my students when I talk to them about creative vision, about the artist's angle. While others are looking up at the night sky, Trimpin has his head cocked to the side, listening; while others may be content to make music within the constraints of existing instrumentation, Trimpin makes instruments that will play the music of the world he hears around him. I want to give it to my colleagues, to remind them that, while we may find intellectual stimulation and challenges in teaching the honors students, the scholarship students, the campus student movers-and-shakers, we can also find joy and challenge and stimulation among those students relegated to what many consider the academic dump. The writing center as junkyard.

As a child, I often spent Sunday mornings with my father and his best friend, Mr. Abby, trash-picking. We'd begin with breakfast and coffee at the Pitt Grill, where my father would run into people he knew but whose names he could never remember. Then we'd drive slowly around town, tapping the brakes as we passed piles outside the neighbors' houses. Occasionally, like Trimpin, we wound up at the dump, but most often we stuck to our garbage-picking drives.

I don't know what became of most of the trash my dad and Mr. Abby rescued on those Sunday drives, but I have come to love the one piece I remember. Driving around one morning, they passed a huge roll-top desk (72 inches wide by 48 inches high by 36 inches deep), coated with the lime-green paint that was popular in the 1970s and covered with muck and crud from having been stored in a shed or maybe even left out to brave the sticky Louisiana summer. According to my dad, he and Mr. Abby couldn't believe their luck, and they rang the doorbell to make sure that the people in the house intended to throw this piece away. Indeed, they did. My dad and Mr. Abby hauled

it off in a borrowed furniture delivery truck, but not before they paid
the man $50 for it. My dad says they couldn't in good conscience take
it for nothing.

Working all summer, the two men painstakingly restored this
piece, slat by slat, drawer by drawer, in the garage behind our house,
until that roll-top desk was ready to occupy the whole back wall of
our formal living room. In a home filled with antiques lovingly
selected and cared for, the roll-top desk, set out to pasture only
months before, became the most stunning piece of all. I was fascinated with it then, for all its secret hiding places and for the textures
on its surfaces, for the rolls that I used to finger like the keys on my
piano. I am fascinated with it still, for those things, but also for what
it represents. And though I no longer visit junkyards or pick trash
from my neighbors' drives, I like to think that some of my father's and
Mr. Abby's sensibility resides in me, that I now spend my days in a
writing center, dusting and polishing and admiring things that my
neighbors might discard or dismiss.

I love Trimpin's vision for its sense of possibility, for his fascina-
tion with what surrounds him at the same time that he fails to settle
for that. What is noise to the townsfolk circling the fire, sounds carried off by the wind, is music to Trimpin, carried in his head into
adulthood. In important ways, Trimpin operationalizes the aesthetics
contained in Luigi Russolo's *The Art of Noises*, penned nearly a century before.[1] Russolo imagined a "futurist orchestra" whose instruments would be built specifically to realize the "six *families of noises*"
characteristic of everyday life in an industrial society (28). While
Russolo's descriptions of the specific instruments and performances
are fascinating, it is Barclay Brown's introduction that provides readers with a sense of the project's significance. Brown, who also translated Russolo's work into English, describes *The Art of Noises* as
issuing forth "a new musical aesthetic," one which has as its thesis, "If
music is sound, why does not music employ all the varieties of
sound?" (2). Composing pieces for this urban symphony necessitated
"the construction of an entire orchestra of incredible instruments
with which to realize that model" (3), an enterprise that consisted of
"twelve different systems of noise generation [with names like 'the

howler', 'the roarer', 'the gurgler', and 'the hisser'], each producing a
highly characteristic timbre" (12). Russolo's crowning achievement,
however, may have been the "noise harmonium, a unification of the
twelve basic timbres within a single instrument that could be played
by one performer" (15).

Russolo and his contemporary F. T. Marinetti were careful to
note, and I feel I should note here, that "the four noise networks
[were] not simple impressionistic reproductions of the life that surrounds us but moving hypotheses of noise music. By a knowledgeable variation of the whole, the noises lose their episodic,
accidental, and imitative character to achieve the abstract elements
of art" (Marinetti, qtd. in Russolo 18). With this quote, I am
returned to the PC memos. Perhaps, for me, the noise of the writing
center has lost its "episodic, accidental . . . character," has become
instead a "moving [hypothesis] of noise music." *F-f-f-ffluidity*, as
Davis might say.

In much the same way, the epigraph from Trinh Minh-Ha that
opens this chapter disturbs the solid state of the lab, the clinic, the
center. It reminds me of how rarely we are inclined to set the gaze
aside—to the extent that we can do so, at least momentarily—and
rely on our other senses, in this case on our sense of sound, for
what it can tell us. Tales of writing centers are invariably tales of
location, of space. They involve a privileging of the gaze. But we
have learned (through feminist initiatives, through multicultural
initiatives, through postmodern, postcolonial, and queer theory)
that the gaze—once posited as objective, as disinterested—is actually quite partial: both limited *and* interested. The perspective of
the gaze, in other words, has been called into question and we
should be searching for ways of representing ourselves *to* ourselves
in partial terms. Paying attention to noise might be one way of
doing so. Where we can shift our gaze, avert our eyes, even (as Peter
Elbow points out) close them altogether, we have no such aural filter. Many of us, I would imagine, talk with tutors about the difference between hearing and listening—the former being passive, the
latter being active—for example. In other words, we receive sound
in an undifferentiated manner—it is disorder; it is chaos—and we

must constantly labor to make sense of the input, to filter and to direct our attention appropriately.

Our writing centers seem clearly to be academic spaces designed to explore the relationship, to exploit the tension, between sight and sound. The memos in the prologue to this book, however, have forced me to acknowledge how very little we say about what we hear or what others hear in the din of our writing centers. Following Trimpin, following Russolo, I think as a result we may be foreclosing possibilities we have yet to imagine. Trinh Minh-Ha writes, "SILENCES are holes in the sound wall/SOUNDS are bubbles on the surface of silence. Sound, like silence, is both opening and filling/concave and convex/life and death. . . . [E]ntering into LIFE is also entering into the DEATH process. Every day lived is a step closer to death and every sound sent OUT is a breaking IN on silence" (203).

What a beautiful image, I think: sounds as bubbles on the surface of silence, as eruptions/disruptions, rising to the surface and returning to obscurity, sound and silence as partners rather than opposites. Silences as momentary risings to the surface of (ambient) sound. Here's Davis quoting Jean-Luc Nancy on this issue: "When a voice, or music, is suddenly interrupted, one hears just at that instant something else, a mixture of various silences and noises that had been covered over by the sound, but in this something else one hears again the voice or the music that has become in a way the voice or the music of its own interruption: a kind of echo, but one that does not repeat that of which it is the reverberation." (2000, 234).

It is these re/surfacings I am interested in: What are they? Where are they? What are we doing with them? Bubbles may burst with the shocking force of a straight pin on a balloon or with the gentle *plink* of a soapy round blown from a child's plastic wand. How do we know what we're listening for?

Nancy Welch writes about breaking in on such silences, on death-work and life-work, in a chapter of her book entitled "Collaborating with the Enemy," a piece she describes as a "chronicle of loss, violence, and compromise" (1997, 37) between Welch (as tutor) and Lee, an ex-marine struggling to make sense of his experiences in the Gulf War.

Welch cites previous work on the teacher-student/Lacanian analyst-analysand relationship (specifically Robert Brooke's 1987 *College English* piece) as "helping [her] to see the process Lee describes of 'opening up' and 'letting go' as trust between [them] being established" (38). Brooke's analysis falls short of illustrating for Welch, however, what to do when that relationship is threatened by "sharp shifts in emotion and attitude." Welch offers a few examples: "As Lee, for instance, hits the brakes, becomes wary of me or his text, or as I become wary of him and his writing" (38). It is worth quoting Welch at length here, as she explains what we might make of such moments:

> Even while our dialogues promise a means for understanding, they can also expose our illusory sense of wholeness and lead us into death-work— the dismantling of that fragile scaffolding of experiences, beliefs, and identifications we experience as self. A student's resistance to this revision-as-death-work is very much a part of the transference relationship. Resistance for Lacan is the mark of a divided self striving to maintain unity and stability even as the self perceives contradictions and gaps— contradictions and gaps that, given the intimate link between language and being, are felt as a death threat. (38)

Welch is careful to note the possibilities these gaps hold, the potential not only for "revelation, revision, and learning" but also for threatening the carefully constructed stable sense of self that student *and* teacher hold dear (39).

The process of revision is also at the same time a process of life-work, according to Welch, *if* we imagine that working together, teacher/tutor and student, might involve reveling in the gaps as productive spaces, might involve a teaching/learning dynamic that is "dialogic, relational *and* interfering and disruptive" (40). Or, to put it in terms particularly appropriate for this chapter, "[I]t's *within* that rhythm of dissonance and consonance, with self-consciousness of the dynamics of control and resistance, that teaching can locate its liberatory power" (40).

The liberatory writing center remains a goal toward which many of us strive, but the writing center also—as has been suggested by

Nancy Grimm, Neal Lerner, and others—can be read as functioning institutionally to *impose* order, to contain the chaotic nature of this otherwise "unruly" mob. In the introduction to her book *Good Intentions: Writing Center Work for Postmodern Times*, Grimm calls writing centers "normalizing agents, performing the institutional function of erasing differences" (2000, xvii). We all know that this doesn't happen: students don't leave here looking any different, dressing any different, having more money, or even, quite frankly, sounding *different enough* to say that writing centers have accomplished this task. Grimm knows this too, and she makes a more persuasive argument later when she describes the function of the writing center not only as a "normalizing [agent]" but as an institutional distancing mechanism for "special" populations: "Because faculty distanced themselves from social change by the very programs they established to manage change—writing centers, at-risk programs, equal opportunity programs—curriculum and teaching methods quickly become out of sync with the changing student population. Serious gaps between the rhetoric of inclusion and the actual conditions belie the appearance that the university has included a new constituency" (9-10).

Writing centers themselves, according to Grimm, are implicated in this distancing maneuver, in the appearance of cleanliness, and she cites writing center professionals' desire to be seen as something-other-than, something-more-than a remedial service as one attempt at such distancing:

> [M]any writing centers distance themselves from a remedial classification by promoting writing centers as places for *all* writers, *not just* remedial writers. The *not just* qualifier was a defensive response to the lack of recognition accorded those who work in writing centers. Thus, the increased diversity of students in higher education is avoided twice—first by universities establishing programs like writing centers that distance faculty from students; and second by writing centers' distancing themselves from a remedial function. (10)

This kind of critique is hard to hear, and I mean that, here in this chapter, quite literally.

When framed as Grimm has framed it, I don't know of one single writing center that escapes the bounds of this critique (though I'm certain once this line is published I will be informed of a few!). Frankly, I don't know how a writing center could. My own doesn't. I have spent my entire tenure at Fairfield challenging the remedial associations of writing center work in part because—why?—it's what we do, it's part of our History, and because it is true enough, I believe, that seeking out response to their writing *is* what writers do—all writers. Yet, when I read Grimm, I am ashamed. And shocked that I had never had the thought before.

HARD (HEADED) NUMBERS: INEFFICIENCY AND WRITING CENTER OPERATIONS, PART ONE

After reading Grimm, I suppose I should be happy to report that my repeated attempts at writing center inclusion have arguably had little demonstrable effect on the actual population of students who frequent the writing center. Most of these students still come (or are sent) because they're having "trouble." The literature on writing centers suggests that this is in fact the case in most writing centers. And, I find it a profound irony that, just as many writing centers shy *away* from their remedial mantles, they are being pulled *into* discussions of institutional efficiency and the efficiency model of operations. It would seem that we are being beaten at our own game.

I fear, sometimes, that we are too willing to give our institutions *what we think they want,* whether or not it is what *we want* or, ultimately, even what *they want.* The shift from remediation to efficiency illustrates this point to me. We take great pains now to highlight in our studies, in our annual reports, the very broad appeal that most writing centers enjoy on our campuses and the cost-effective manner in which we operate. Most of us, for example, are advised to include in our annual reports *hard numbers* (As opposed to soft numbers? Or easy numbers?): number of students served (Do you want fries with that?), number of students from each course, from each major, from each year, from each school, always-another-from-each-that-I-seem-to-have-forgotten. Is this what we do? No. But do we do it? Yes. And we do it for "good" reasons, I suppose, though I don't feel like writing about those. What I do feel like writing about is what happens when we mistake *doing it* for *what we do*—and when our colleagues, administrators, and occasionally our tutors and students, follow us in making the same mistake. I feel like thinking about what happens when we fetishize the numbers of students we see from every end of campus, the numbers of hours we've worked, the numbers of students we've helped to retain for so comparatively little cost, *rather than* what happened during those hours, between those students. It is rare that annual reports—my own included—tell stories of the latter.[2]

It seems we instead feel we have a lot to prove—to whom, I wonder—and yet, we have never proven quite enough. Enough!

A worrisome trend, for example, appears to be one Muriel Harris lays out in "Preparing to Sit at the Head Table," part of *The Writing Center Journal's* twentieth anniversary issue. In that issue, authors were invited to respond to three questions:

> Given changing educational demands, populations, budgets, and technology, how do you see writing centers continuing as viable parts of the academy?
>
> In what ways will writing centers continue to be viable contributors to the research community?
>
> Can you target any issues that writing centers need to open up or begin to address that have to do with our future place in the academy and the larger community? (DeCiccio and Mullin 5)

Responding, I imagine, to question three, Harris observes that online tutoring companies (like Smarthinking) pose a threat to the continued operation of the individually supported writing centers we've come to know and love (and depend on for our livelihoods). Anticipating arguments against the outsourcing of writing center work, Harris notes, "Several studies have already shown us that writing center tutoring works in terms of grades (an overt sign of success in many circles)" (18), and she cites studies by Neal Lerner, by Stephen Newmann, and by Craig Magee, all of whom independently determined that students who used the writing center had better grades than those who did not (or in the case of Lerner, performed "as well as students who had SAT verbal scores over 200 points higher!") (qtd. in Harris 18). I feel torn. I am glad to know this, happy that someone is interested enough and knowledgeable enough to do this research. But I am also troubled by reports like these. I do not agree with the premise that we need to learn to speak administratese to be heard in our universities, nor do I agree that speaking it acts as a talisman against initiatives like the outsourcing of university work. I do not intend to have conversations like the one Harris anticipates above. At least, I don't intend for them to follow that same trajectory. I was, in fact, disappointed to read this passage so soon after I had argued successfully to our university outcomes assessment committee that grades are *not* an appropriate measure of a successful writing center session, since better grades might simply mean, for example, that a tutor overtook the session, and since poor grades do not necessarily mean that the student did not benefit from the exchange. Instead of implementing this measure, we decided on a more qualitative method of assessment, involving focus groups, that seemed to please the committee and that will also provide, in my opinion, a richer description of our work. If the quantitative, "bean-counter" mentality provides us with an answer that (we think) administrators *would like to hear,* whether or not it reflects what *we* believe to be important about the work of the writing center, I fear we may not look for an/Other way out of here! A way that might even (*gasp!*) leave everyone reasonably satisfied.

Harris's solution, and the research she cites to support it, is an example of what Harvey Kail, writing in that same issue of *The Writing Center Journal,* calls "'value added' research, in which we try to measure the development of student writing in relation to writing center sponsored interventions" (27). While acknowledging the importance of this research, Kail urges himself to move beyond it, to follow North and John Trimbur, both of whom have "issued intriguing calls . . . for research that emphasizes the writing center as a window into the unique conversations about reading and writing that abound there" (27). The sticking point? We all know it: Time. As Kail writes, "[I]t is late in my day when I get around to thinking of the writing center director as the writing center researcher—very late in the day" (27). In what he describes as an "only slightly exaggerated" manner, Kail lists his priorities as "teaching, service, service, service, service, and then research—on our service" (28).

At the small, private university where I work, every faculty member whom I respect feels beleaguered at one time or another by the amount of service he or she feels compelled to perform. I don't think that the situation Kail describes—one which I'm sure elicited knowing smirks from every writing center director who read it—is particular to us. I think it is specific to faculty who take their jobs, and consequently the health and integrity of their universities, seriously. While it may be attractive to imagine that such (over)work is solely our province, I simply don't think it's the case, and I question where we think this depiction of ourselves gets us.

At the 2000 National Writing Centers Association meeting, Neal Lerner refuted his earlier study (on which Harris relies) in a presentation entitled "Choosing Beans Wisely."[3] In his introduction, Lerner revealed "an embarrassing truth: my study was flawed both statistically and logically."[4] The published version of his talk offers a detailed critique of those flaws, especially the problems with the assumption that low SAT verbal scores are highly correlated with poor performance in first-year composition. Lerner observes, for example, that "the relationship between SAT math and Expository Writing I grades is actually stronger!" (3). All in all, Lerner views his article as a "cautionary tale," one which he hopes will discourage the view that writing center directors are "little more than the ticket tearers at the writing center turnstiles" and will instead "link writing center outcomes to larger writing center values and theories, as well as to college/university-wide goals" (5).

I am encouraged by the care with which Lerner sets out to raise and respond to important questions about our work (and by the strength it takes to turn such a critical eye on his own), yet I was disappointed that Lerner's audience for this work at the NWCA conference in Baltimore included so few people. More participants at that same convention were present, I'm sure, to hear Molly Wingate's

keynote address, which provides an interesting counterpoint to
Lerner's argument. Wingate provided more value-added research for
the audience to consider. Her talk began with this thesis: writing centers contribute to a culture of academic seriousness on their campuses. Her evidence: statistics gathered (primarily) recording the
GPAs of writing center clients (along with some more informal comments about the academic strength of the tutors). Apparently, writing
center users have higher GPAs than non-writing center users. There
was more information that washed over me, I'll admit, partly because
of a bacon-induced stupor (it was early) but partly because I was disappointed. Wingate first had the unenviable task of following Cindy
Gannett's heart-wrenching, beautifully-constructed tribute to Bob
Connors. But I know Molly Wingate to be someone invested in
what's-so-funny-'bout-peace-love-and-understanding, and I was
hoping for something, I don't know, different. I was not expecting so
clear a turn to the rational/e.

During the Q-and-A segment, audience members seemed focused
on whether or not these stats would be made available to everyone.
Would she be publishing them, for example? Wingate graciously
agreed to provide them to people, but then backed off any claims to
statistical rigor by admitting that these numbers were collected fairly
unscientifically, that she's no statistician, that one of her assistants
had in fact questioned their validity shortly before Wingate left to
give this address. She downplayed the "seriousness" of the assistant's
concern by pointing out (rightly) that no one in the crowd would
really *care* about such pretensions to statistical validity (or if they
cared they certainly wouldn't call her on it). I was left with the
impression that the writing center's contributions to academic seriousness were perhaps some sort of . . . game. If we're *just* "playing" at
academic seriousness, shouldn't we admit it? Had she just done so?
Why can't we talk about *that* bold move?

When those sitting at our table turned to speak to each other, at
Wingate's request, about "bridges and barriers" to our own writing
center's academic seriousness on our campuses, Carol Haviland
admitted that she thought their writing center was "too much
devoted to academic seriousness." I had to agree.

As my husband and I planned our wedding—my second, his third—I found myself wondering whether Samuel Johnson's wry observation about remarriage as the triumph of hope over experience would make for an appropriate toast. (Ultimately I decided against it.) I see this same triumph repeated over and over again in our service work, in our drive to quantify what it is that writing centers actually *do*. Much of this work may seem—may actually be—necessary, but very little of it has resulted in a real shift in the nature of our "institutional viability" (Brannon and North 2000, 9). When we do research on the relationship between grades and writing center attendance, on the relationship between writing center attendance and GPAs, I have to wonder whether this is research *we* really care about or whether this is research we think *administrators* really care about. (Wingate's presentation certainly suggests the latter, to me at least.) Like Kail, it is late in my day (some days) when I manage to do the research I really care about. I can't tell you how nearly impossible it is to find time to do the research I *don't* really care about. Maybe you already know. Somehow it seems there's *always* something better to do than that. I'd rather imagine doing the research I care about and then *persuading* others that this is the research *they* should care about, since that research is (presumably) one of the reasons I was hired to do this job.

Though we hold out hope that the typical calls for more research in/from the writing center should change (perceptions, funding, status for faculty), somehow they seem not to have the desired effect. Instead, they threaten to merely reduplicate the noise of the institution. Like the closed feedback loop I will describe later in this chapter, such value-added research may serve simply to return the noise back to the institution, unchanged. You want us to demonstrate broad appeal? Just look at all the students we saw from all these different classes and all these different majors. You want us to demonstrate efficiency? Just look at all the students we saw from all these different classes and all these different majors. Just look. Just look. Just look.

But does anyone hear?

HARD (HEADED) NUMBERS: INEFFICIENCY AND
WRITING CENTER OPERATIONS, PART TWO

I am reminded of Trimpin when I drop my annual report into
campus mail and send it (flying). Then I can cock my head to the side
and (*shhhhh*) listen—to the tapes of tutoring sessions, to the tales
my notes tell (or don't tell) about the previous year, to the tutors'
voices on the phone when they call to ask for references or to talk
about jobs for which they're applying, to Hendrix and, this summer,
to Lou Reed. (Thanks, Dave.) To summer days and swims and bike
rides. To inefficiency.

Early last fall, I received a call from the coach of the women's basketball team here at Fairfield, asking if we could set up group tutorials
with several of her players who seemed to need particular—what?—
help, ummm, attention, (academic) motivation? Without some significant assistance, these women were in danger of being deemed
ineligible to play. Some of them already were. Before I gave the
request much consideration (in retrospect, of course, I should have
given it more), I agreed to work with her to e-n-c-o-u-r-a-g-e the
players-in-question to meet with Katie, a recently-graduated Fairfield
alum doing a stint in the writing center for a year. Katie is bright,
approachable, articulate, funny, a student who has retained a remark-
able intellectual curiosity despite having had more than her share of
academic difficulties. Katie, I thought, is the one for this job.

Katie met with each of the women throughout the year—in pairs,
in small-group sessions—at assigned times and at other times. By the
end of the year, a couple of them had stopped coming, and Katie had
figured out to stop calling them, but several of them seemed to represent the kind of success stories we like to tell at orientation or at lunch
or at other public forums where we're supposed to tout the writing
center's effectiveness, the kind that figure neatly and cleanly into the
research Harris writes about—research on grade correlation; on
retention; on dedication, motivation, and improvement. The story of
Katie and the Basketball Players turned out, on the face of it, to be
uncomplicated and unsurprising. Except for Angela.

Angela arrived for her first, for her second, for her third appointment in the writing center with no books, no notes, no syllabi, with

apparently no work to do at all. Angela stood out, quite literally, on our campus. Angela, in fact, stood out even among her peers on the basketball team. She towered over Katie, who at 5'11" herself was no slouch. Though Angela was first scheduled to work in a small group with two other teammates, her resistance was sabotaging the work of the others, so we scheduled her for individual appointments with Katie. After each meeting, Katie would walk into my office and shut the door. We would strategize. Katie carved up her requests so that, by the end of one meeting, her only request for the next session was that Angela bring a book, any book, whether she had read it, was reading it, was supposed to read it or not. Before that meeting, Katie and I discussed options. We both considered it meaningful, in some way, that Angela actually showed up for the meetings, though we didn't quite know what meaning to assign to her attendance. And we agreed that Katie needed to fill the hour in some way so that Angela wouldn't think that her failure to arrive with any work would actually turn into the reward of her early departure from the session. We both resented the position in which we found ourselves, as disciplinarians, complicit with someone's agenda other than the student's. We also felt, however, that simply giving up on Jessica was somehow not the solution, either. That seemed to be what she was expecting, what she was waiting for.

Instead, Angela learned something she couldn't have known to expect when Katie revealed during one of their meetings that her own academic career had been punctuated by failures, both course failures that were the consequence of a learning disability and career failures that were the result of her inability to secure a place in any of the graduate programs to which she had applied. Everyone was surprised by this admission: Angela, of course, because she could not and would not have known otherwise; Katie, because she had not planned to disclose these very personal details; and me, because I was nervous about the direction the sessions would take from that point on.

At their next scheduled appointment time, Angela arrived with books in hand and with a list of assignments she needed help completing. I could offer in greater detail the triumphalist narrative of

Katie's and Angela's sessions: the one where Angela receives her first *A* ever on a paper and comes bounding into the writing center to share the moment with Katie, exclaiming that she can't wait to tell her parents, even though she doubts they will believe she did all the work herself; the one where Angela discovers that she really likes her psychology class and decides to major in early childhood education; the one where Angela's grades climb high enough to qualify her to play basketball for the first time in her nearly three years at Fairfield. I could tell this narrative because it really did happen. I could even include Angela in the kind of end-of-semester grade correlation Harris talks about.

But then I would have to figure out what to do with the rest of the story, with the part that has Angela looking at schools other than Fairfield, where she had never fit in; that has Angela researching schools with programs in her newly-declared major (which Fairfield doesn't offer); that has Angela transferring mid-year to a larger state school, one where she could maybe get lost in a crowd once in a while, one with a better basketball team *and* an early childhood education program. It is a narrative worthy of an academic satire, really. It is also, I think, a tremendous success story, at least to the point where she left Fairfield. But it is not, obviously, a story I share with many of my colleagues. It is not a story that would make many administrators happy. It doesn't write the writing center as a mechanism for university retention. Yet I take great pleasure in having watched these events unfold.

Angela was sent to the writing center, to be sure, to have her signals straightened out, to have her attitude adjusted. No one would have anticipated this outcome. Even though we don't tell stories like this one very often—we are more apt to tell the ones that position the writing center as *contributing to* university retention efforts rather than *detracting from* them—stories like these are frequent enough, even in our own writing center, to make me wonder what other stories are not being told. So I am suspicious of the neat, clean, efficient research like that on writing center-letter grade correspondence because I suspect it actually tells us very little at the same time that it fails to tell us a whole lot.

TURN IT ON—AND ALL THE WAY UP

Katie's and Angela's meetings were not efficient. In fact, a full twenty percent (is that a hard number?) of their sessions, as near as I can figure, focussed on absolutely no writing at all—not Angela's or anyone else's. This, to my ear, is the noise of the writing center: Noise in the system is considered extremely inefficient. It is disruptive, an interference in the clear, harmonious well-ordered transmission of information. It is something (usually) to be *gotten rid of.* When we concern ourselves with how to transmit information from sender to receiver in the most efficient manner, with the least possible distortion—with, in other words, the least amount of noise—we are constructing a theory of dialogue that *depends upon the exclusion* of a third party, whose contributions are dismissed as mere static in the system, whose mere presence is deemed unsanitary. What—or who—has been sacrificed in this straightening out/up becomes a serious issue.

Does this sound like our university system? How about a theory of education that *depends upon the exclusion* of a third party? Does this sound familiar?

Critics such as Michel Serres (1982), N. Katherine Hayles (1988), and Jacques Attali (1996) contend that this "efficient" transmission of information results in a system that is endlessly iterative, redundant, repetitive. These same theorists have rescued noise, arguing that the exclusion of this third party amounts to the exclusion of genuine information. In fact, these theorists argue, order develops *out of* chaos, not through the elimination of it. Moments that threaten the stability of a system are also moments that may, in the words of information theorist Eric White, "provoke systemic transformation" (1991a, 94). Ironically, it is the noise, not the official information, that allows for the mutation and potential reorganization of the system.

How about the writing center as a place where people seek out the genuine information that might otherwise be suppressed or eliminated? As a place powerful enough to allow for the mutation and potential reorganization of our system of education? These are not rhetorical questions. I really believe the writing center is that place. And if you are working in a writing center, if you are "supporting" the writing center at your own institution (however you might define that support), then you had better believe it too.

The final chapter of this book will consider what such moments of systemic transformation might look like. In the end, they appear less revolutionary than we might imagine. They are, in fact, the kinds of interactions that we see every day in our writing centers, the exchanges that should give us pause but often don't. For now I will merely point out that "microscopic random fluctuations—purely chance occurrences—can bring about macroscopic transformation" (White, 1991b, p. 263). The sum total of those microscopic fluctuations—movement produced by reading a memo from a colleague, by mindlessly arranging magnetic poetry only to discover that it has relieved a writer's block, by swapping a favorite film with a frequent writing center client—results in a sort of institutional (over)growth.

Paying attention to these microscopic fluctuations may also mean, however, admitting that our writing centers are (uh-oh) extremely inefficient. Let me be the first to admit this about our own operation here at Fairfield University. The Total Quality Management types would have a field day with our operations. I have refused, am continuing to refuse, to be pulled into conversations about the efficiency of the educational system. Efficiency is a bad model for the growth and development of the human mind. When I read my students' literacy autobiographies, they never write about how *quickly* they can get through a really good book or how *few* extraneous words their favorite ones have. They write about their special places to stretch out and linger over those precious last few chapters, about the smell of the children's library at storytime, about a conversation with a friend that led them to discover a new author. These experiences fly in the face of efficiency, thankfully. Such moments baffle the "practical" tutors of Emily Meyer and Louise Smith (1987). These moments are not replicable. They are simply happenings.

Discussions of the institutionalization of the writing center often focus on the ways in which and the degree to which the academy echoes within the walls of the center, rather than on the ways the center might amplify, even distort, the noise of the academy. PC might have expected that his memo would be one instance of such an echo. He might have imagined that I would use it for support, as back-up, in trying to maintain (or regain) control, to impose order on my tutors (as if they are *mine*). He probably did not expect that I might use it to turn up the volume on some of the difficulties the tutors and I have faced in doing this job. Or that it could even be used to tout some of our successes. Or—*horror!*—to champion even less traditional ways of teaching and learning than what he witnessed here that night. He probably did not expect that I would read his memo as an invitation to talk back to him and to others on my own terms. I see this move as an amplification of the noise he instigated. He might view it as a distortion. It is, in all probability, both of these things, and I see them both as being good.

It is in the spirit of amplification that I return to my argument with Leahy's piece, to the suggestion that committee work and/or a sabbatical for the director result in the suffering of the writing center, for example. These suggestions, and those like them, smack of narcissism and of co-dependence. At the risk of invoking the very nurturing, maternal overtones to which I object, I wonder why we don't imagine that our occasional absence might be *good* for the writing center, that it might be *healthy* for us to take a break from each other, the same way that parents (especially mothers) are encouraged to "carve out" a little time for themselves in that *Good Housekeeping* sort of way. Leahy's comments seem designed to make us feel *guilty* for leaving our babies in the care of others.

I have had occasion to experience, in the last several years, the particular benefits accrued by two of the mechanisms Leahy singles out for criticism: applying for tenure and taking a sabbatical leave. While I am well-aware of the dissension among the writing center ranks regarding faculty/non-faculty status, I will not debate the issue here. I will point out, however, that these same two mechanisms have resulted, for me, in some of the most productive exchanges I've had with colleagues.

In graduate school, Mark Hurlbert, who was then teaching a course called *The Politics of Composition Instruction* and who later directed my dissertation, returned to our class after break one Thursday evening toting a box nearly as wide as he was tall, and probably as heavy. In it were his tenure materials. As I recall, most of us were too intimidated to do much more than circle the box curiously and maybe flip through a header or two, giving it only the most cursory examination. It seemed so personal—years' worth of evaluations from students, years' worth of publications, letters of recommendation from colleagues near and far, proof of service on this-or-that committee. Our class traveler and good friend Ann Ott later described it as "a box of blood" (Ott, Boquet, and Hurlbert, 1997, 165). The box loomed large over the class that evening, and I'm sure we asked questions about the process, though I don't remember anything specifically. I suspect no one, including Mark, had anything good to say about the whole experience, short of being happy that it was over. I remember feeling that the road from there to here—from graduate school to tenure—seemed long and daunting and not quite real.

The road has, in fact, been long and daunting but also very, very real. And, like Mark, I am happy that it is over. Several things about having applied for tenure and promotion, however, cause me to think differently about this process now, to consider it as more than something to be gotten through, something other than simply a hurdle to be jumped.[5] Gathering and preparing the materials takes a long time—years for the gathering and months for the preparation. I tried hard, most days, not to resent the process, to view it instead as an opportunity to reflect on my time at Fairfield and to educate those who would see the materials on the work of the writing center. It was a lofty goal, and many days I didn't accomplish it—days I spent trying to set up a grid to summarize my student evaluations, afternoons I spent looking for a missing syllabus or two—but some days I did manage it. Writing the Statement of Case for Tenure and Promotion was eye-opening in a lot of ways as I began to make sense of where *I* fit here at Fairfield, not just where *the writing center* fit. Organizing my materials forced me to admit that I have a role here in the life of this university *independent of* the life of the writing center, and that (more importantly) the writing center has a life at this university *independent of* me. Somehow that seems as it should be. So committee work and service work and teaching do not take me *away* from the work, as Leahy apparently perceives they do in his case. These things, in fact, more fully realize the work of the writing center to the extent that they allow me to more fully participate in the life of the university.

Waiting to hear—now, that's another matter. October to April. Running into colleagues on the committee in the hall, in the dining room, at meetings, wondering what's been said about the quality of your work and, by extension, you. Paranoia. But the waiting seems necessary and inevitable. And one day, you get The Word.

Soon after the letters went out, but before any official celebration had commenced, I received a call from a colleague with whom I had a passing acquaintance—friendly, but we'd never had much contact—and who had been one of the members of the Rank and Tenure Committee. He called to tell me that he had been "blown away" by my application. He had in fact had no idea that the work of the writing center was so fresh and invigorating and, well, interesting. He felt it was "cutting edge stuff" and asked if we might get together and think about ways that we could drum up more support for the writing center, since he had figured out, without my ever explicitly saying so, that we didn't have the resources to be an all-revolutionary, all-the-time writing center.

Nearly two years have passed since that initial phone call, and the relationship we've developed has been mutually beneficial, I hope, without being demanding. We have worked on proposals for more writing-center space, as well as for more writing-center funding. We are trying to imagine something really different, some sort of transdisciplinary work, without being quite sure what that means. But we're thinking. And sometimes we just have lunch. But that's important. In the meantime, I feel he is a powerful advocate for the writing center, helping me, for example, to strategize ways to think about assessment that make sense to me as well as to our administration. He has never asked me for a statistic, for "proof," for a breakdown of anything, even when he functioned as an administrator. Knowing that he understands and supports the work of the writing center makes it easier for me to be here and to do this job. And that is important too.

For the purposes of this book, he is also my link to Hendrix, main-lining info about feedback and amplification when I have needed it. A killer musician with a theory-head. What could be better?

But his office is in the Other college, on the Other side of campus, and I'm not sure we would ever have had an/Other occasion for contact, Other than this one.

Post-tenure: I am now fully vested, I suppose, in this university, and I have been awarded the time this semester, as I mentioned earlier, for sabbatical research, to write this book, which I have been trying to write for the past four years. It is now August, several weeks before the official start of my fall sabbatical, yet already I have seen two important-though-not-necessarily-anticipated outcomes from this impending leave. The first involves research I proposed as part of the sabbatical project, a study of the staff meetings at the Rhode Island College (RIC) Writing Center, which is directed by Meg Carroll.

Nine years. That's how long it had been since I spent any time in a writing center for which I was not responsible. This summer, I spent several days each week doing the assigned readings and writing for the RIC staff meetings, conferencing with Meg and the tutors in charge of coordinating the staff meetings, and participating in paired and group discussions and activities. Truth be told, I didn't know how badly I needed to do such a thing until I did it. To participate in the life of a writing center and not be in charge of, oh, let's say, the payroll, the supplies, the scheduling, the public relations. I had not realized how heavily these details weighed on my experiences in my own writing center until I was relieved of them for a while. (I run the risk now, I realize, of invoking the very nostalgia I seek to critique.)

I am not suggesting that, during my time at RIC, I was "just" a tutor. I know better than that. I am, however, suggesting that there is no way out of the administrative role the director plays in her own writing center, even if, for example, she regularly sits down with a student to tutor, as many of us do; even if she participates in cross-curricular efforts and committees across her own campus. And while the administrative component of the job is necessary and important, few of us, I would imagine, chose to spend our careers in writing centers because we wanted to *administer* them. We chose to spend our time in these centers because we appreciated (and continue to appreciate) the richness of *tutoring*. But, to paraphrase Kail, it is late in the day when we quit thinking about ourselves as administrators. That, I think, is unfortunate.

So spending time in the RIC writing center was nice. It was just nice. And it was important. An added bonus lies with the fact that Meg and I gathered loads of good material and had a really wonderful time.

Before beginning the RIC project, I was required to submit a summary of my proposed project to the RIC Human Subjects Review Board in order to secure their permission to conduct the research. The board meeting came up in a hurry, and neither Meg nor I spent much time thinking about the text of the proposal. We just got it done.

Meg's position at RIC is defined as part-time administrative staff, converted from the full-time, tenure-track faculty position that it was when John Trimbur held it in the early 1980s. Her goal before she retires is to get it converted back. Like most part-time writing-center directors, hers is a full-time job and then some. Over the last several years, Meg has been active on the regional board as well as on the national board, and she has hosted the regional conference. Her undergraduate tutors routinely attend and present at the Northeast Writing Centers Association Conference, at the National Conference on Peer Tutoring in Writing, and for the last two years at the Conference on College Composition and Communication. Her administration? Well, we're sure they appreciate it.

We really never imagined that the submission of our project proposal would begin a buzz on her campus about the writing center's clout; and yet, it has made the rounds, with board members actually approaching Meg about the research taking place in the writing center, with bits and pieces of the document showing up in annual reports and in performance evaluations. We are left to wonder what the effects of the published research will be. We are hoping it might be a significant piece of the evidence necessary to convince her administration that the writing center needs more support than it currently receives. Of course, the research might not have this effect. But if it does, the RIC writing center has gained a lot; and if it does-n't, no one has lost anything. In fact, no matter what, Meg and I and the tutors and maybe even some students still come out ahead. All of this is to say that perhaps we need to think more broadly about the impact of time for research, time for committee service, time for sabbatical leaves and tenure preparation.

Meanwhile, back at the ranch: no doubt there have been logistical problems. I have learned, for example, that it takes someone who is much more organized than I am to turn over this operation to someone else for a semester. As a result, I have not managed to let go of the writing center entirely during my sabbatical—I'll admit that. Mariann Regan (the colleague whom I have pressed into writing-center service during my sabbatical) and I have set up weekly meetings to stay on top of the writing center's operation (though we wind up meeting briefly more often than that); and I have agreed to attend staff meetings when I can. Mariann began, late in the spring semester, attending my staff education class and staff meetings with me, as well as reading the course materials and current research. All of this has taken a bit of coordination on both our parts. But Mariann is the person who had the idea for this incarnation of the writing center at Fairfield in 1981, and she is a thoughtful and considerate colleague who has been a member of the English department for nearly thirty years. So I feel fortunate to be able to leave the writing center in her care. That is a luxury, I realize.

And yet, it is strange to walk into the office in the morning and see Mariann sharing bagels with the tutors. It is alienating to receive copies of flyers to faculty and to students with her name on them, to read email messages from her to the tutors. I have resisted the urge several times already this morning to go out there and see what they're laughing about or why it suddenly got so quiet. With the door closed, I can hear them talking but I can't quite make out what they're saying, and I wonder if it's something I should maybe know. Or something I could maybe help with. Or something . . . I don't know. The more uncomfortable I am with all of this, the more I realize I need to step back from it.

In conversation with Mariann, I ask her to talk to me about her impressions of directing the writing center—a very different writing center—again, after all these years. I admit to her that I'm having difficulty letting go (as if she hadn't figured this out already), and we joke about this. She gently suggests, "As I understand it, letting go is what the philosophy of the writing center is about." She adds, "Freedom of inquiry is not a one-person job; it is a many-person job." This line, in my opinion, should rank right up there with North's "our job is to produce better writers, not better writing" as a mantra for writing center staff.

Obviously, having Mariann in the writing center is already good for the writing center. She has managed to accomplish things that I have put off. She is a different voice articulating the same needs: more space, a new computer, recognition for the tutors and acceptance of the writing center philosophy. Today, she asked me whether she should know anything specifically as she prepares the budget for next year. "Don't ask for more money," I tell her. "Ask for more space." She casts a glance around the crowded room and nods in agreement. "Do you mind if I try talking to a few people about this?" she asks. Mind?! Mind?!

In the midst of all her excitement, Mariann has also been nervous about her new role in the writing center, and she has been very open in admitting this to me. I have been less open about my own concerns about having her in the writing center, concerns wholly unrelated to her level of competence. I have complete confidence that she can do the job admirably. But I'd be a fool not to worry that she might do the job better than I. She very well might. In fact, I think she can, and I hope she does.

This writing center is not mine to (dis)own. I find myself having to renegotiate this relationship I thought I had with *my* center, with *my* tutors, with *my* colleagues. An identity in crisis.

Noise has us reimagine the relationships between the writing center and the academy, relationships like those I've begun to complicate above. Noise asks us to consider how and where the writing center echoes throughout the institution. Making noise might be a one-person undertaking, but it can also be a many-person undertaking. And the many-person version is quite likely to yield different results. In either case, noise positions the writing center as a site of amplification and of feedback rather than merely as a (waste) receptacle, though such feedback may result in pain as often as it results in pleasure. And sometimes the two emotions (pleasure and pain) are inextricably linked, in a hard-labor sort of way.

WOULD YOU PLEASE TURN THAT DOWN?: FEEDBACK AS PAIN

At a mom-and-pop Jamaican restaurant at our final-Friday-lunch-before-the-students-return-for-the-year, our colleague Malcolm is having difficulty following the conversation at the table. Olivia gets up to ask the owner if he would turn down the "background" music. Malcolm's wife April explains that Malcolm can't hear, and we joke that this is the result of standing too close to the stage at all those Pixies concerts. We joke, but it is probably true. My mother was right: we have gone and ruined our ears.

Every once in a while, I still manage to go to a concert or two. I paused at a local club concert recently to note that nearly everyone was wearing earplugs. The members of the band were; the members of the road crew were; even people in the audience were. I felt so . . . naked. Exposed. And terribly, terribly retro. First no sunscreen and now this.

I've paid to see moderately forgettable, appropriately obscure bands at dark, stinky clubs all over the country, and I could always count on one thing: at least once during every show, someone on the stage would forget himself just long enough to position the source too close to the amp. Then, like fingernails across a chalkboard magnified a thousand times, came the unmistakable screech, squeal, and howl. Microphonic feedback. Ouch.

The audience's response at these moments is predictable (at least it was before earplugs): people slap their hands to their ears, scrunch up their shoulders, contort their faces. It's instinctual. So while micro-phonic feedback itself may not be inherently interesting (as is, say, harmonic feedback, which I take up later in this chapter), the primal nature of the audience's reaction actually is. Microphonic feedback reminds me that feedback, if we're not careful, can be quite painful.

This semester, we have seven new tutors, all of whom have taken the staff education course and all of whom have, as a result, spent a great deal of time thinking about appropriate feedback to give to writers when they arrive. Enough of this talk and we might forget that writers often have *already received* feedback by the time they get to us. Many times that feedback has been quite painful, the type of feedback that causes them to slap their hands over their ears (or at least over their papers) in an attempt to retreat from this allegedly communal experience and fold into themselves instead. Once they begin working in the writing center, the tutors never forget this for very long. They don't have that luxury. They know instead that they can count on a steady stream of students whose end comments may include a profes-sor's wry observation that "paragraph 12 was a *delightful* surprise, in that it actually made sense" or otherwise helpful hints, such as this simple one offered by a faculty member in the English department: "Learn how to write." Thanks. We'll get right on that. And, by the way, you've just made the job *sooooo* much easier.

Tutors know too that they are vulnerable to this type of feedback as well—more so, perhaps, because they, of all students, are sup-posed to "know better." More than once, a tutor has questioned whether she can be of any help to other writers when she can't seem to get a handle on her own work. One particular tutor, whom I found sitting on the couch, staring blankly at the wall, told me of a difficult meeting she had just had with a professor, discussing the rough draft of one of her own papers. In his initial comment, scrawled alongside the student's introduction, the professor advised, "One should never begin a paper with an introduction that is boring and lacking in content . . . which you have successfully done." [Ellipses are the professor's own.] This tutor and I talked for a bit, and I assured her that I wanted her to continue tutoring in the writ-ing center. She agreed, but then she asked whether she had any appointments scheduled for that afternoon. "I don't want to help anybody today," she muttered.

For many of us—certainly for me—the writing center is most interesting for its potential to transform the system. I am suspicious, however, of the language of transformation within our universities—and certainly within our writing centers—a language that is celebratory, jubilant—like butterflies drying their wings in the spring. After moments like the ones recounted above, with tutors, with students—with Todd—we have to be wary of such language, I think. Noise rather insists that transformation can be quite violent (though it is not always and doesn't necessarily have to be). I am reminded of Toni Morrison's trilogy (*Beloved*, *Jazz*, and *Paradise*), a trilogy exploring violent social cleansings and the function of the sacrifice—to provoke disorder and then propose order. To say, See how much better it is once things return to "normal"? Noise works against the idea of normalcy—the writing center as a place to bring aberrant students into line; the scripted session that takes a disorderly student/text and orders it into a pretty (dull) paper; the faculty member who claps her hands to her ears and pleads with us to make it stop. At best, such moments should not be considered normal; at worst, they hurt.

I can't write myself out of this section, knowing as I do that I have surely included comments on student papers that were ambiguous, unsupportive, maybe even mean. I don't intend to indict others without indicting myself. Only last semester, in the second half of our first-year English sequence, I grew increasingly frustrated with a class that repeatedly refused to engage multiple interpretations of a text we were reading. Finally, after the seventh student offered essentially the same interpretation as the previous six, I stomped my foot, whirled around from the blackboard, and yelled, "*Why* do you all *insist* on assuming that the main character is male?" There was, to my mind, an air of jesting to the question, but when I saw the face of the student who had offered the final comment, the one that prompted the outburst, I instantly knew it had not come off that way. She was a quiet student who sat in the back of the class—I was a loud teacher standing at the front of the class—and her freckled skin was now marked by bright red blotches. I apologized profusely to her in class and explained that I had meant the response to sound more light-hearted than it did. I also sent her an email message to the same effect. She said, "It was no big deal." Of course. What could she say? What can I say about an event like this? So much and then nothing, really. Just when I think I'm past it . . . Persistence, not perfection, I suppose.

This summer, while cleaning out my office, I dug through the artifact drawer, the bottom drawer in my corner file cabinet filled with materials I will almost certainly never use again but which tell me something about where I've been in this profession. There's a dialogue journal from Don McAndrew's Teaching Writing class at Indiana University of Pennsylvania, letters of acceptance from grad school, a memory book put together by high school students and counselors in the Rural Scholars program that Ben Rafoth ran, a copy of my first contract from Fairfield. At the bottom of the drawer are several student papers from the first English class I ever taught, a basic writing course that I planned shortly after the semester I worked in the writing center with Todd. It is a random assortment of essays, made up apparently of assignments never handed back because students were absent on the day they were returned. Each paper is handwritten and neatly folded in half. My comments appear beneath the student's name and beneath the oversized, red-letter grade. Jim Caldwell's essay #11 rated an F and the comment "good paper, but 3 major errors." Good paper, but here's your F? Who is this woman? Maida Alexander's paper was also an F. Hers too warranted the assessment "still not passing but your papers have improved." Improved to an F?! Russell Alvins made an F due to "major and minor errors—past participle endings on verbs. Also, the 3 things you listed *cannot* be traditions." I open the papers, hoping to find more thorough explanations written into the text itself, but I know I won't. And I don't. I discover, instead, a bold, red ? across one whole paragraph and annotations like "verb form" and "R-O." The one extended comment in Russell's text merely parrots the assessment on the cover: "These are not traditions. Look up the definition of a tradition." I cringe as I recall that class: the men who missed every other week because of their seven-days-in/seven-days-out work schedule on the oil rigs. Women who showed up to an 8 A.M. class still in their hospital scrubs, having worked the night shift, coming to school before going home to see their kids, to have some breakfast, or even to get some sleep. My throat burns, and I can't bear to look at these papers anymore.

PUT A SOCK IN IT: FEEDBACK AS POSSIBILITY

Technical Tip of the Day (11/06/98): Have you ever noticed that once you get the equalizer tweaked it is usually the open strings that still tend to feedback or ring out of control? Try to dampen the strings a little bit. Just a little bit of felt on the close side of the nut (not the tuner side) will help a lot. One guitarist I know used to lightly tie a sock around the neck at the nut. He claimed that the sock helped to minimize feedback and helped to clean up some slop in his playing. (Sweetwater Sound, insync.sweetwater.com)

In the interest of full disclosure, I will admit that I don't play the guitar very well or very often, though I long to, and I alternate between toughening the pads of my fingers and relegating my Ovation acoustic/electric to the bowels of my basement when it serves as too painful a reminder of my technical (in)expertise. It is much the same with my writing.

Picking up my guitar, as sitting down to write, is a curious mix of an overwhelming sense of possibility and a crushing admission of my own limits. Music and writing—both remind me that inherent in the concept of possibility is an understanding of limits. Possibility is a word that gets thrown around with abandon in our educational circles, but it doesn't hold up very well to scrutiny. Educational possibility seems nebulous to me. What does it mean, really? Ultimately nothing, I think. It lacks any sort of intellectual reference point. The limit: now there's a concept with which we can all identify. Limits are appealing then (at least in analytical terms) first because they are quite tangible (though that is also often their frustration) and next because they force us to identify, even focus on, particular transcendent *moments*, make those specific trangressions tangible and real as well. Davis writes, "this writing [of which Davis has been writing] will have been written . . . not to give or address anything *to* others but to expose the limit—'*not the limit of communication, but the limit upon which communication takes place*' (Nancy, *Inoperative* 67) . . . [A] genuine writing is 'the act that obeys the sole necessity of exposing the limit' (67). Writing is the singular gesture of touching that limit and so of *reaching for others*" (Davis 239).

Each day that I sit down to write, I am scared. What if people hate my book? (They will, Hurlbert says.) What if it makes people mad? (It's supposed to, Hurlbert says.) It is Davis, though, who explains to me why I feel so ex/posed. (Where are those earplugs when you need them anyway?) I write in an effort to touch the limit. And in doing so, I inevitably expose my own limits as well. Nancy Welch once joked to me, as she awaited the publication of her book, that she wished to write in the preface, "No reviewer need point out to me the short-comings of this book. I can list them all myself."

Yet, we write. She . . . and I . . . and you . . . and our students. We write because in "touching that limit" we simultaneously "[reach] for others." I wonder how often we teach with that in mind. What are we doing, in our classrooms and in our writing centers, with the hands that students are extending to us? What do our hands look like to them? (*First do no harm.*) I am consistently amazed, given remarks like those listed above, that students continue to write, not only when writing is assigned, but also when it is not. The biggest surprise of last semester came from Scott, a senior soccer player enrolled in my staff education course. Because he was graduating, he knew he would never be a tutor, but he wanted to take another writing elective because he thought he needed more "help" with writing. He was self-conscious in the class, often making self-depre-cating remarks about being one of the only business majors in a sea of English major faces. Yet he presented to us, as part of the work on his literate life history, the class's most interesting document: a chronicle (some might call it a journal) of every soccer game in which he had ever played, from pee-wee league straight through his senior year of college.

While all our students surely possess the capacity to be surprised and delighted (and to surprise and delight us as a result), writers arrive in our classrooms and in our writing centers with clear ideas of their own (discursive) limitations. Process theorists have expended a great deal of energy learning to talk to such writers, teaching them to talk to each other and to themselves about their writing. Process theorists have spent a lot of time, in other words, considering the feedback writers receive. Nevertheless, we are left with a paradox: For all our talk about the recursive nature of the writing process—the seemingly endless loop of revise and resubmit, revise and resubmit—our discussions of feedback presume a singularly linear, uni-directional strategy. Appropriate feedback, in other words, moves writers toward more controlled, more tightly-woven, more highly-organized products. In practice we know this not to be the case, yet the rhetoric of limitless possibility implicit in our discussions of feedback prevents us from considering what are, in fact, its very real discursive limitations. Thinking about this leads me to consider feedback's other life—in music.

I return again to PC's memos, specifically to the idea that what gets labeled as noise is essentially a value judgment, a means of dismissing signals as chaotic, disruptive, meaningless, uninteresting. So when PC refers to the work taking place in our writing center as "noisy," it means he doesn't hear what I hear. It means he's not listening the way I'm listening. He has, effectively, *written off* what those writers have to say, how they say it, and what he might actually learn from it.

I can consider our differing interpretations, PC's and mine, of the institutional function of a writing center in feedback's musical terms. His as a place where such noise should be contained, where signals should be straightened out. Mine as a place where not nearly so much control is exerted, where signals may occasionally come squealing back at us or may go howling off into the stadium.

Admittedly, PC's understanding is probably consonant with most institutional desires for the writing center, at least since the 1970s. Writing centers proliferated then and now largely because they seemed to hold the promise of containment—squirrelling away certain student populations (athletes, international students, minority populations, remedial students). What institutions didn't bargain for, though, is that housing these student populations as such might result not always or even necessarily in containment but in *amplification,* in reverberation, might actually turn up the volume on the kinds of demands that students make on institutions of higher learning and might send institutional dictates and mandates screeching and squealing back to their source.

> Distortion: ANY deviation in the shape of an audio waveform between two points in a signal path . . . The more harmonic distortion there is, the more the sound will begin to take on the quality we call "distorted." (Sweetwater Sound Website)

"The Sound of Silence: Vote on Noise Ordinance Draws Nearer" reads the headline of the September 22, 2000 issue of *The Mirror,* Fairfield University's campus student newspaper. This article is the latest installment in a series chronicling the ever-worsening relationship between Fairfield-student beach residents and year-round beach residents. If town residents get their way, after this vote, a students will be responsible for paying $100 each time a police officer is called to respond to a noise disturbance at the student's residence. At the most recent town council meeting, town resident Colleen Sheriden showed a home video of the "'close to 2,000 student revelers in [her] neighborhood [Saturday] night'" (qtd. in Coffin 1). Responding to Sheriden's videotape and to the impending vote, Tim Healy, the Fairfield student representative on the town beach association, says, "Tensions at Fairfield Beach are now at the highest point they have been in at least the last two years."

I admit I derive a perverse sort of pleasure, as I write this book denouncing the academy's (in)tolerance of noise within its ranks, from seeing my own university embroiled in noise battles on several fronts. As Fairfield University continues to fight this beach problem to its south, we are also facing litigation from neighbors to our north, a new subdivision (that has gone up on property the university sold explicitly for that purpose) only yards away from the university's townhouses (where some juniors and seniors live) and abutting our new artificial-turf practice field. Currently, the field cannot be used after 6:00 P.M. or after dark (whichever comes first) because the lights bother the neighbors, and the subdivision is pressing the university to construct a noise barrier to block disturbances from the townhouses.

"Practice Noise Control" reads the sign posted on the gate of a local swimming pool. The juxtaposition of *noise* and *control* strikes me as odd at first, until I pick up that copy of *The Mirror* and realize that "noise control" is getting to be serious business here at Fairfield. The university is dumping lots of money into this effort—new residence halls (to discourage students from wanting to live at the beach), more money for on-campus programming (to discourage students from wanting to *go* to the beach), a university beach officer to deal with town residents' complaints. And yet they can't quite keep it under (w)raps.

The official position of the university on these matters is one of sympathetic indignation. The unofficial position, heard when members of the university community discuss town residents complaints among themselves, is less tolerant, tending instead to portray town residents, in their beach cottages and McMansions, as having distorted the issue of noise control.[6] The president himself, in his end of the year address to faculty, "concluded that the University was engaged in a public relations war with a small group of neighbors . . . who [were] ably assisted by the local press. Statements [were] exaggerated, students [were] harassed, and outright lies [were] accepted unchallenged by reporters" (Minutes of the Meeting of the General Faculty, May 9, 2001). Healy, interestingly enough in the article cited above, recognizes this same strategy and riffs on it a bit when he accuses town residents of "[amplifying] the tensions."

Distortion and tension are intimately related. In fact, distortion in music is often described as "tension release," as "grit." Yet feedback in writing is expected to be the opposite of distortion. Elbow, for example, writes that "[c]riterion-based feedback helps you find out how your writing measures up to certain criteria" and "reader-based feedback tells you what your writing does to particular readers" (1981,

240). In both cases, writers are left with no room to imagine that feedback will do anything but help them to "clean up some slop" in their papers.

What Elbow imagines here is what's known in systems theory as a closed feedback loop. A thermostat provides the simplest, typical illustration of such feedback. The thermostat is set to a certain temperature—say, 70 degrees. When the temperature in the house drops below 70, the thermostat sends a signal to the furnace. The furnace kicks on and remains on until the thermostat registers 70 again, at which point the thermostat sends a signal to the furnace to kick off. Etc. There is little room for instability in this particular type of feedback loop, short of total system failure. There's nothing random or unpredictable or particularly exciting about this type of feedback. It is very controlled, task-oriented, directed. But it is *not* the only type of feedback we might talk about.

We might also talk about harmonic feedback, which is the type of feedback Hendrix made famous (and is famous for). Here's how it works: when an electric guitar is plugged into an amplifier, the string sound is converted to an electrical impulse. When the string begins to vibrate, the feedback loop begins. The amplifier makes the sound of the string louder. When the sound produced by the speaker hits the string, the string begins to vibrate more. Those vibrations are returned from the amplifier and, if conditions are right, the sounds get louder and louder and louder. The other strings begin to vibrate in sympathy, which is picked up by the amplifier and then they get amplified. And so on, and so on, and so on. You can see how this might quickly get out of control.

Before Hendrix, the only possibility most musicians might have imagined when this happened was to get rid of the feedback.[7] First to prevent it, if possible. Next, to get rid of it. But Hendrix didn't try to eliminate the noise. Instead, he embraced it for its randomness, for the possibilities that this feedback afforded, and he improvised by playing melodies *against* the feedback, by playing rhythm *and* lead.

Once you have the bottom there you can go anywhere.
That's the way I believe. Once you have some type of rhythm,

like, it can get hypnotic if you keep repeating it over and over again. Most of the people will fall off by about a minute of repeating. You do that say for three or four or even five minutes if you can stand it, and then it releases a certain thing inside of a person's head. It releases a certain thing in there so you can put anything you want right inside that, you know. So you do that for a minute and all of a sudden you can bring the rhythm down a little bit and then you say what you want to say right into that little gap. It's something to ride with, you know. You have to ride with something. (Jimi Hendrix, qtd. in Hatay 106)

As I work on my writing this morning, I hear the tutors working with students in our writing center right outside my door. I hate to admit this, but 9 times out of 10, having worked with these tutors for a year or two years or three years, I can predict how the session is going to proceed: how the tutor will begin the session (by having the writer read the paper aloud), how the interaction will be initiated (by asking the writer some version of what-do-you-want-to-work-on-today), and how the session will move from there (Michelle favoring beginning with the thesis, Katie by talking about development, Kristy by determining what the writer knows about this particular writing assignment).

Gilles Deleuze writes, "[R]epetition is attributed to elements which are really distinct but nevertheless share strictly the same concept. Repetition thus appears as a difference, but a difference absolutely without concept; in this sense, an indifferent difference" (15). T. R. Johnson, who directs the writing center at the University of New Orleans, offered this interpretation of Deleuze's thesis in *Difference and Repetition*, a summary which I can match for neither its clarity nor its brevity, so I will simply repeat it here: "What's forever reproduced is difference" (Personal correspondence, September 30, 2000). We acknowledge this about writing centers when we champion them as sites for individualized instruction: the scene remains the same, but each session is different.

The sessions differ in part because the tutors differ, one from the other, in spite of their often all-too-obvious similarities. (Our student population here is, on the face/s of it, quite homogeneous compared with other universities, and our writing center staff is more homogeneous still.) As even my sketch of their sessions demonstrates, these tutors obviously did not internalize a script to such a degree that they all even approach a session the same way with a student. I don't know why they begin where they begin—maybe because they perceive their own strengths lie in different areas, maybe because they interpret students' needs or desires differently. For whatever reason, they begin where they begin, and their beginnings are not the same beginnings from one to tutor the next, though they are often the same beginnings from one session to the next.

I couldn't responsibly suggest that we operate without a script all the time or that we have no sense where we might want a session with a writer to end up or how we might imagine getting there. But it's difficult to advocate even a loosely-scripted approach, for myself and for my staff, without seeing us eventually caught in a feedback loop that becomes less and less about limitless possibility and more and more about modulation and control, where the revise and resubmit cycle becomes an endless process of reiteration and redundancy, increasingly contentless. Along with that comes a recognition that such work creates its own brand of discontent, among writers and responders. Where is the pleasure? Where is the fun? Where is the place where writer and respondent can enter into a groove for that session?

The lockstep repetition of much of our advice to tutors ("Begin by asking the student what he or she would like to work on") and consequently the lockstep repetition of much of their practice, threatens to mask *what* gets repeated each time. The Hendrix quote above, in contrast, encourages us to find space for potential *within* that repetition, to search for those gaps. Trinh Minh-Ha writes,

> Repetition as a practice and a strategy differs from incognizant repetition in that it bears with it the seeds of transformation. . . . When repetition reflects on itself as repetition, it constitutes this doubling back movement through which language (verbal, visual, musical) looks at itself exerting power and, therefore, creates for itself possibilities to repeatedly thwart its own power, inflating it only to deflate it better. (190)

Here Trinh calls for *purposeful* repetition, opening up a different class of strategy for those of us who work with tutors. Repetition-as-strategy differs from the pre-emptive strategies too frequently offered as palliatives to tutors, occasions where we offer *solutions* to *problems* tutors may not have even encountered yet. Language that looks at itself offers a different sort of mirror for tutors (and students) than the traditional mirroring model affords.[8] This mirroring model considers what it sees *in its own reflection* and plays with it—makes a strawberry, sticks out a tongue, watches with detachment as its face dissolves in tears. Whereas the previous mirroring model sought to conceal the gaps, gloss over them with verbal volley, parrot back student questions and concerns to them, a self-conscious tutoring strategy using repetition would "[set] up expectations and [baffle] them at both regular and irregular intervals. It [would draw] attention, not to the object (word, image, or sound), but to *what lies between them.* The element brought to visibility is precisely the invisibility of the invisible realm, namely the vitality of intervals, the intensity of the relation between creation and re-creation" (191).

I occasionally visit writing centers at other universities as part of an assessment/accreditation team. At one visit, I met with a tutor who described the bulk of her sessions to me: tutoring thirty students from a film course, all of whom had written film reviews on one of the two movies that had been playing in town that weekend. "How do you deal with that?" I asked. "It helped me to talk to the professor," the tutor replied. "He told me he wanted the students to develop their papers more. So when they come in, I know what to tell them." "What do you say to them?" I asked. With a quizzical look on her face, she finally shrugged and replied, "I tell them to develop their papers more." No doubt she told them more than that. She probably talked to them about *how* to develop their papers more. The point, however, remains the same: it is difficult, especially in the face of the kinds of pressures tutors face with each session, to move tutoring practice from rote repetition to fresh challenges. To be blunt, it is just plain hard work.

Can we follow Hendrix, I wonder, in using such repetition in productive ways? Repetition-as-strategy opens up an otherwise closed system by becoming attuned to complexity. In doing so, repetition brings the noise forward so that it might become, in Eric White's words, "a force for renewal" (1991b, 268). This is that "certain thing" inside a person's head to which Hendrix refers. Here's White again: "Though noise may destroy one system, this destruction permits the emergence of another, potentially more complex system in its place.... As order comes out of chaos, so sense requires nonsense. Meaning emerges not as predictable derivative but as stochastic departure from tradition, as *invention*" (1991b, 268).

Hendrix's music (and his career) make evident the manner in which moments of transgression can grow out of such repetition. The key, perhaps, lies in how we *experience* those moments.

Hendrix was all about *Experience*.

May this be love or just confusion born out of frustration of not being able to make true physical love to the universal gypsy queen of true, free expressed music. My darling guitar . . . please rest in peace. Amen. (Jimi Hendrix, eulogy, written on the back of the Fender Stratocaster guitar that he smashed at the end of his farewell London performance, June 4, 1967, www.jimi-hendrix.com).

This was caught on tape: Hendrix smashing and burning his guitar at the end of the Monterey International Pop Festival in June of 1967, his American "debut," two weeks after the performance I just alluded to in London. At the end of the performance, Hendrix takes his guitar, smashes it and burns it before an audience who looks, for the most part, (dazed and) confused. What most people in the audience didn't know was that this scene was staged, had in fact been played out before, two weeks earlier. When I first watched the Hendrix performance on video, this destruction didn't make sense to me either. Guitarists love their guitars. They're weird about them. B. B. King ran back into a burning building to rescue his Lucille. Janis Ian puts a "please return—no questions asked" clause on every one of her discs to this day, hoping to find her Martin D-18 #67053 that's been missing since 1972. Hendrix slept with his guitar. His fellow squadron members in the 101st Airborne used to play keep-away with Hendrix's guitar, as Hendrix followed them around the base on his hands and knees, begging, sobbing, pleading for its return (Murray 1989, 36).

The Stratocaster Hendrix smashed in London was already cracked along the back when he wrote his eulogy on it. Once I discovered this, what appeared to be a random act—one out of character for him, it seemed to me—began to make sense. He wraps up this powerful performance by sacrificing his instrument, dancing around it, conjuring up its spirit from the flames and releasing it into the crowd, *presiding* over this noise that he had just created.

In contrast, when Hendrix smashed and burned his guitar at the Monterey Festival, his American debut, he was already caught in a closed feedback loop of sorts. Once his fans saw what he could do, they wanted him to do it again and again and again. "Purple Haze" at every performance; the "Star-Spangled Banner," which Hendrix reinvented, simply repeated over and over and over; an uninspired encore performance of "Wild Thing" tossed in at the end of his New Year's Eve Performance at the Filmore East. Murray (1989) writes, "[T]he fresh material seemed to be merely tolerated by the audiences, who reserved their most enthusiastic applause for the traditional crowd-pleasers. Both his management and his audiences seemed determined that Hendrix should be content with simply repeating his former triumphs" (55). An A & E Biography on Hendrix shows an interview clip of Hendrix, shortly before his death, remarking that he's "tired of doing the same stuff" and expressing the hope that his fans can "come along with [him] to the new stuff."

There's so much I want to do—I want to get color into
music. I'd like to play a note and have it come out a color . . .
in fact I've got an electrician working on a machine to do that
right now. (Jimi Hendrix, qtd. in Hatay 109)

Having lunch with my favorite associate dean, who in his other life has a joint faculty appointment in business and religious studies and who in his *other* other life is a kick-ass lead guitar player. I was bouncing some of these ideas off him, about Hendrix, about the writing center, and he was bouncing them right back. At one point in the conversation, he said to me, "What if it's not sustainable? It seems to me you have to allow for the possibility that this sort of thing just can't be sustained. Hendrix couldn't sustain it."

I'm not sure that Hendrix couldn't sustain it. Maybe his pathetic, tragic death is evidence that he couldn't. But maybe he just died. Maybe he just died. We know he didn't die because he ran out of ideas. We know that he could imagine—that he *was* imagining— much more, was re-inventing the studio as he had re-invented the stage, was not above using bottles and cans to improvise a slide to achieve the *exact* sound he heard in his head, or constructing a kazoo out of a comb and Saran Wrap to lay over his track of "Crosstown Traffic."

We too need to think about sustainability. But I also know that part of what sustains me is the idea that I might re-invent a moment with a student. And that enough of those moments might mean that I have eventually re-invented the idea of a writing center on my campus. And that enough of *those* moments might mean that I, along with others, have re-invented the way such work gets valued *beyond* my campus. Deleuze sees repetition as "the fundamental category of a philosophy of the future" (1994, 5). Given that repetition seems inevitable in the writing center (as in the rest of life), how are we using it to imagine a more challenging, fresh, productive future for ourselves and for others?

Jacques Attali, the economist/philosopher/musicologist, has defined music as "the organization of noise" (1996, 4). I hear most clearly the link between noise and music in feedback, both literally (as in Hendrix's stuff) and figuratively, as I work with writers. And I'm prepared to imagine that thinking of feedback in this way might lead, eventually, to a greater tolerance of distortion, to a recognition that there exists an element of distortion at play in every interchange. And to imagine that we can grow to tolerate it, that we might even learn to like it and seek it out. Play (with) it. Riff on it a bit. That we might think of feedback not as a relay from point to point to point but as sympathy, as harmony, as vibrating independently and in tandem, like the strings on that sacrificial Fender guitar.

FEEDBACK AND WRITING CENTER "EXPERIENCE"

In the September 1999 issue of *College Composition and Communication (CCC)*, Nancy Welch writes about the importance of *play* in the writing center in an article entitled "Playing with Reality: Writing Centers after the Mirror Stage." Welch describes a tutor's work with a student named Sun Young, who comes to the writing center as a self-described non-writer and presents herself as "hopelessly blocked" (58). When the tutor presses her on these points, asking Sun Young to respond in writing to questions that encourage her to characterize herself as a writer, the tutor learns that Sun Young does in fact write poetry. From there, poetry becomes a vehicle through which Sun Young and her tutor can explore other texts and Sun Young's own writing. Theorizing from this narrative, Welch uses the work of child psychologist Donald Winnicott to consider the importance of play in the writing center. Winnicott writes, "Play is neither inside nor outside" (Winnicott, qtd. in Welch 59). Welch follows, "Instead it takes place *within* the tension between inside and outside, between desire and demand, in an 'intermediate area of experience' between subjective and objective realities'" (59).

As I read this sentence, I am struck by the musicality of it, not so much by the rhythm of the prose (though that is certainly admirable) as by the tenor of the ideas. The best analogy I can find for *play* in the writing center, for investigating the relationship between (job) performance and pleasure, is the one of improvisation in music.

As the previous Hendrix quotes suggest, improvisation is largely about repetition, repetition, repetition. It is also a consequence of expertise, of mastery, and of risk. The first thing a musician learns about improvisation is that it is *not* anything goes. Improvisation is instead a skillful demonstration performed by someone who knows the tones of her instrument, the rhythms of her musical traditions, so well that she can both transgress and exceed them, give herself over to them, play within and against the groove. The most interesting improvisations work because they are always on the verge of dissonance. They are always just about to fail. They are risky. But when they work well, they are also really, really fun. They leave you wide-eyed.

When is the last time you took a risk during a session with a writer? Writers, after all, risk a lot coming to us. What are we risking in return? When is the last time you could characterize a session as really, really fun? Today, I hope. Maybe so. But if not, why not?

As I write this, I am preparing to meet and greet the seven new tutors beginning in the writing center in two weeks. They would be quick to remind me that they are risking a lot too, and they would be right. I do not mean to diminish the anxieties tutors feel about their qualifications, their capabilities, their own academic records, their obvious and not-so-obvious differences (whatever those may be). I do, however, mean to disturb their carefully constructed shield of strategies.

I have risked a lot in this book (or at least it feels that way to me) in part because doing so seems only fair, given what I am asking, but also because it seemed like that was the only way to enjoy it. The work is too hard and the process too long not to have fun doing it. Writing this book has opened up a new area of conversation between the tutors and me. Though I am on sabbatical, I write daily in my office, and I take (frequent) breaks from my writing to emerge with a new favorite quote for the board, gleaned from a book I've been reading. I print out pages and bring them with me out onto the couch to get a perspective not afforded by my computer screen, scrawling notes in the margins or longhand (Luddite that I am) on a legal pad. When they ask, "How's the writing going?" I hope that my responses capture the complexity of a task as challenging as this one is as well as the enjoyment that I derive from those challenges (even when they frustrate me). One of them said to me, "It's really cool that you're writing a book." Yeah, I guess it is.

I want them to think that their jobs are really cool, too, and I believe most of them do, once they begin tutoring. But I struggle with how to get that component of the job across to them early on. I fear losing them in a semester-long training course that seems designed to dictate the "practicality" of the job, to "guide" them (like a seeing-eye dog) through their sessions. I am unhappy with a model of staff education that sets up a content model for tutoring, a low-risk/low-yield approach to staff education. Such a model frames the guiding question as "What do tutors need to know in order to be effective?" and training sessions are organized around such concerns as steps in writing a research paper, how to clarify a thesis, and how and when to document sources.

It's easy to see how this model for staff education developed. Writers come to the writing center often with seemingly specific needs: Write a research paper. Clarify a thesis. Tutoring to those needs can produce a competent session that proceeds along a fairly typical trajectory. By predicting what writers are likely to *need* in a session, we imagine we can forestall problems by preparing tutors to address those needs. We can give them *experience* with those *types* of sessions. This makes a potentially frightening occasion seem less risky, right? Here's how to begin the session. Here's a good question to ask after the student has read the paper aloud. Here's a good question to ask if the paper doesn't yet have a thesis. This is a very disciplinary model: It makes tutoring appear as a content area to be mastered. It assumes that gaining experience is the same thing as acquiring expertise. And it downplays the amount of risk involved in doing this work as well as the kinds of risks one might need to take in order to find the work meaningful, fulfilling, even pleasurable.

Two moments have come together that cause me to complicate this low-risk/low-yield model of staff education for myself and for my students. The first involves the inevitable question I face each semester after presenting a list of stock methods and stock responses (like the ones I mentioned above). Invariably someone asks, "What do I say once the student answers?" My only response was (and still is) well, that depends. Not a particularly helpful response, I've learned.

One recent work that addresses this issue is William Macauley's "Setting the Agenda for the Next Thirty Minutes," the opening chapter in Bennett Rafoth's collection, *A Tutor's Guide: Helping Writers One to One*. Rafoth writes that he asked contributors to follow a set organizational pattern for their articles: Introduction, Some Background, What to Do, Complicating Matters, Further Reading, and Works Cited (ix). I confess to turning, in each essay, first to Complicating Matters.[9] The suggestions in the first three segments are familiar and echo what readers might find in any other manual. Macauley writes, for example, "Setting the agenda for the next thirty minutes . . . will most likely be a variation on this general framework: review the assignment, decide on the goals for the session, and finally, choose the best route to reach these goals" (4). This, we are to understand, is our map, which may need to be negotiated and re-negotiated throughout the session. Macauley offers observations in the Complicating Matters section, however, which provide key insights into the problems with a strategy-oriented approach to a tutorial. He writes, "Though mapping a tutorial is a very smart way to begin, the work of a tutorial is often not predictable enough to allow that map to remain essential throughout the session. Second, if the map becomes cumbersome, drop it. As I said before, the map is only as good as it is useful. *Sometimes, it is better to explore than to plan*" (7, my emphasis). The students in my staff education would surely want to ask Macauley, as I do now: *then* what?

The second moment of dis/ease for me involves the dissonance produced by Elbow's loop writing exercise, one of the first writing activities I assign in any of my writing courses (including my staff education course). Here's what Elbow has to say about the loop writing process:

> The loop writing process is a way to get the best of both worlds: both control and creativity. . . . I call this process a loop because it takes you on an elliptical orbiting voyage. For the first half, *the voyage out*, you do pieces of almost-freewriting during which you allow yourself to curve out into space. . . . For the second half, *the voyage home*, you bend your efforts back into the gravitation field of your original topic as you select, organize, and revise parts of what you produced during the voyage out. Where open-ended writing is a voyage of discovery to a new land, the loop process takes a circling route so you can return to the original topic—but now with a fresh view of it. (60)

Student writers often have a difficult time voyaging out, and Elbow's loop provides a helpful way of talking with them about what it means to prematurely foreclose possibilities in our writing—a reminder that we can't return home until we have ventured away and that the ad/venture re-frames our sense of home.

Every semester, before teaching the staff education course, I review the training (wheel) texts available to tutors. And every semester, as I try to decide whether to use any of these texts in the course, I wonder, where in these texts do the *tutors* get to "voyage out?" Davis writes, "[I]t may be time to stop offering *more* pedagogy or *altered* pedagogy in answer to the failure of pedagogy. . . . Here we will not attempt to inscribe yet another pedagogy into the pedagogical scene. We will hope, rather, to EXscribe ourselves, to locate a postpedagogy, a pedagogy that would be other/wise . . . *a pedagogy of laughter*" (2000, 213).

So I want to suggest that our current taxonomy—the research paper session, the thesis session—does an injustice to the principle we claim to hold nearest and dearest to our writing center hearts: that the benefit of the writing center is the personalized attention, the one-to-one work with writers that we can provide. The low-risk/low-yield model changes the scene in which a directive is given—the teacher gives it in the classroom, the tutor gives it (maybe friendlier, maybe more collegially) in the writing center—but it doesn't fundamentally alter the writer's relationship to the material, as Sun Young's tutor did with her.

The obvious question here is, at least as I see it, what would a different model for staff education consist of? How might we develop a model that encourages tutors to "voyage out?" The different model that I am working toward—and I'll be the first to admit (and I'm certain my tutors will back me up) that we're not there yet—is a higher-risk/higher-yield model for writing center work. The first step involves those of us who work with tutors (and I'm including at least some measure of faculty support beyond the director of the writing center): we need to recast our understanding of the nature of experience so that we might think of it, in terms of training, not as something someone "gets" (so that peer tutors always fall short when compared to graduate students who fall short when compared to professional staff who fall short when compared to faculty, etc). To think of experience not as something that someone either possesses or doesn't but instead as something which is continually constructed and reconstructed.

This higher-risk/higher-yield model asks us to reformulate the question "what (or how much) do tutors need to know?" and to cast it, instead, in more musical terms: how might I encourage this tutor to operate on the edge of his or her expertise? And, for tutors: where is the groove for this session? Where's the place where, together, we will really feel like we're jammin' and how do we get there? Where, as Welch has framed it, is there space for play?

I fear that a low-risk/low-yield model for tutoring encourages a framework of mere competence, of error-avoidance. I don't want tutors to fear mistakes—because they *will* make them. The real skill lies in figuring out what to make of those mistakes. I don't want tutors to choose the safe route rather than (maybe) the exceptional one. I want them at least to *try* to exceed the mean expectations that they hold for themselves (and that perhaps others hold for them), even if such attempts result in their occasionally falling below those expectations. So I am suggesting here that we need to reject the institutional demand that the writing center produce institutionally competent tutors who help to produce institutionally competent writers. I think we do our tutors a disservice when we "train" them in ways that suggest that we are more concerned with their being competent than with their being truly exceptional—which will involve some horrible moments, no doubt. And I think we do our students a disservice when we don't allow them to see our growing pains, our own intellectual struggles, challenges, and successes.

3

TOWARD A PERFORMATIVE PEDAGOGY IN THE WRITING CENTER

A memorial service for a famously self-destructive performance artist is about to start, and out on the sidewalk on the Lower East Side, the sousaphonist for the Hungry March Band is teaching the tenor sax player a new song.

No sheet music is required.

"We're going to repeat five notes," Scott Moore, the man with the big horn, tells Emily Fairey. "The first three notes everybody drew out of a bag, different notes for everyone. The fourth note is a collective B flat. The fifth note is your choice. It's sort of a tribute to his idea of random chaos."

Ms. Fairey nods like a veteran pitcher. "Got it."

Newman (1)

My friend Geoff arrived for a visit on a Sunday afternoon and went straight for my guitar. "I heard this song on the radio on the way down here, and I want to play it for you," he said. "I think you'll like it." He smiled gently as he plucked the strings along the neck, shy as always about inviting a demonstration of his musical talent, and then he rendered the song perfectly without exactly reproducing it. I was so jealous I could hardly breathe.

I am a literate musician. I never played a note until I had learned to read it, and now I can't play it unless I can see it. A terrible musical handicap. Perhaps this is why I resist to such a degree the idea of scripted performance in the writing center. I much prefer thinking of the work of the writing center as random chaos, or maybe controlled chaos, instead. It is a frame that enables me, in my work with writers, to acknowledge the importance of preparation while at the same time immersing myself in the pleasure of the here and now. But that of course means that we have to consider the here and now in all its glory as well as with all its dents and scrapes. *Oompah.*

Coming clean about the chaotic nature of our work is no doubt troublesome to some people. In fact, much of what is written about the work of the writing center (and, for the purposes of this chapter, much of what is written in the way of advice to new tutors) touts the orderly nature of our work, plotting the writing center, as I have already written, on a triumphalist trajectory of improved grades, improved retention, established protocols and procedures, and reasonably replicable methods. (See also my February 1999 *CCC* article for more on this.) In this way, we—those of us who re-make our writing centers on a daily basis—are as implicated in the containment of our practice as are the administrators, faculty members, and institutions we work with (or against).

Our work is, of course, not without order, nor should we want it to be. But from whence is that order derived? If the writing center is to function as an apparatus of educational transformation, that order must develop *out of* chaos, not through the elimination of it. We must imagine a liminal zone where chaos and order coexist. And we would certainly do a service to ourselves, to our students, and to our institutions if we spent as much time championing the chaos of the writing center as we do championing the order.

This tension between chaos and order is most evident to me when I sit down to plan my annual staff education course. Getting materials together for the course, which I teach every spring, coincides ironically with what is perhaps the most chaotic point of our writing-center year—halfway through the fall semester.[1] Over the past six years, I have taught the course using almost all the staff education manuals available for tutors. I have used Ryan's *Bedford Guide for Writing Tutors,* a slim volume offering bare-bones advice to tutors, along with Harris's *Teaching One-to-One: The Writing Conference.* I have taught with Capposella's *The Harcourt Brace Guide to Peer Tutoring* and with Murphy's and Sherwood's *The St. Martin's Sourcebook for Writing Tutors,* a text designed to ground potential tutors firmly in composition theory and to provide traditional readings (like North's "The

Idea of a Writing Center") to bring students into the professional conversation. This past year, I used Gillespie's and Lerner's *The Allyn and Bacon Guide to Peer Tutoring*, a manual that fills out the sketches offered in a text like Ryan's and offers an ethnographic approach to the study of writing-center tutoring. Two other texts that seem promising are Reigstad's and McAndrew's *Tutoring Writing* and Rafoth's aforementioned *A Tutor's Guide*.

This is the chronicle of a professor dissatisfied with the course she has been teaching.

Each of these texts has accomplished its basic task—that is, enabling a tutor to sit down with a student and talk about a piece of writing—reasonably well. The authors of these texts are all well-respected writing center professionals. Semester after semester, however, students rate the texts as "not helpful" and I find myself unhappy with the material presented in them. Many tutors, for example, will not need a chapter entitled "Getting to Know the Student." They get to know their peers all the time. Who am I to presume they need direct instruction in this? (In fact, many of our students might point out that—whoops!—we're the ones most in need of this sort of instruction.)

I look at these collections, with book titles that dictate the practicality of the job (e.g., *The Practical Tutor*, Meyer and Smith 1987), with chapter titles like "Analyzing an Assignment," "Finding a Focus" and "Organizing and Developing a Draft" (chapters four, five, and six of Capossela) and I am b-o-r-e-d!!! Though these are all important issues to discuss with writers, I wonder about foregrounding their significance, about strategies appearing so early in the texts, and about play and experimentation being so . . . well . . . absent. Why aren't these books more fun? How do these texts represent the work of the writing center to the potential tutors? How and where do they prefigure the mutation, potential transformation, and re-organization of our systems of education? As far as I can tell, they don't. But they should.

In defense of myself and in defense of these texts, I would say that this is a difficult course to teach because it needs to accomplish several important tasks: it must get tutors up-to-speed with their own

writing; it must encourage them in shaping a philosophy of education, of teaching, and of learning; and it must help them to figure out
ways to think usefully (and quickly) about responding to the work of
their peers and about enabling their peers to respond to their own
work and the work of others. Those are big jobs for one course.
Labeling it a difficult course, however, glosses over the fact that all
courses have multiple charges and face numerous challenges. Calling
the course difficult also downplays what I know to be true: this is my
favorite course to teach.

Articulating a vision for this course has boiled down for me, in the
last few years, to stepping back from the class/work and asking, "What
do the sessions in the writing center look like?" and "What do I *want*
them to look like?" Designing the course then becomes a process of
figuring out how to get from point B to point A. Following Bruffee and
North and Trimbur, I feel strongly that writing-center sessions are not
substitutes for faculty response or supplements to classroom instruction. Sessions in the writing center have their own, let's say, groove. I
began listening closely to what my colleagues were saying about the
work of their centers and learned that people like Denise Stephenson
and her tutors at Grand Valley State University use toys and manipula-
bles in writing-center sessions. I heard Frankie Condon and Mike
Condon issue challenges to writing center directors that our centers
become models of non-violence and sites for the interrogation of race
and privilege. I was also fortunate enough, through sheer geographic
proximity and overlapping terms on the Northeast regional writing
center board, to sneak a peek at Meg Carroll's tutors, only to discover
that they were doing the work that I wanted to see take place in our
writing center. Much of this chapter, then, describes the meetings I
observed during a summer-long study of the staff education program
at Rhode Island College. Putting into place such training involves
working to make the exception(al) the norm in the writing center.

Describing the course in detail, as I am about to do here, means
that I run the inevitable risk of scripting and sedimenting what I wish
to remain unscripted and unsedimented. Failing to describe the
course would, I fear, leave me open to the fair question of what this
theory I have laid out would actually *look like* in practice. I prefer to

chance the former. I do hope, however, that the following trans/script will be taken in the spirit in which it is offered: not as a pre/script-ion to cure the tutor-training blahs but as observations, exaltations even, of the performances of the players in one particular writing center during particular moments in time.

THE PLAYERS (in order of appearance)[2]

Mike: I'd like to say that in the past few months I have been gaining a wider perspective of the globe . . . learning more from listening than ever before, unsure of tomorrow but endlessly hopeful. I am learning more and more that our actions and words effect change in everything and everyone around us. Through careful and compassionate analysis of the spectrum of possibilities, our movement through this world can be both positive and enriching.

Jill: Senior English major. Can be sarcastic in the best way possible. Most polite and quiet loud talker ever. Initiator of discussion in journal book.

Meg[3]: One groo-ooo-oovy lady; generous with her mind; persistent tutor recruiter! Keeps me straight on birthdays; has the best sunken living room ever; the horse loving, button losing, organized director.

Lisa: The quiet, thoughtful tutor who constantly pursues knowledge and always types papers in show-all-characters mode.

Justin: I guess I am not a typical tutor. I became a tutor before my senior year at RIC. I enjoy working with people and communicating with them. . . . I have learned a great deal about various different types of people during my short stay here in the WC.

Bryan: Bryan is a writer with his moon in Pisces. He makes crazy mix tapes for his friends and loved ones and currently resides wherever his friends will set him up.

Sarah: Sarah is the summertime absentee training woman, but be assured while absent, she is battling for justice—not the American way.

Amy: Amy Peters entered the writing center as a fourth year student in part-time study of English and philosophy. Two years later, she left as a wife and mother. In that she married a fellow tutor, she feels she owes much of her happiness to the enchantment of the WC.

Joanne: The girl who said 'crap' . . . distracts others from their homework with tales about Gramma . . . knows just about every song on the radio.

Donna: I am the mother of two brilliant children. I am an artist. I guess that's it—I don't think a lot about myself.

Barbara: Barbara was our videographer who, as a theater major, is usually much more at home in front of the camera. Since she's been to all the meetings, she thinks she'll apply to be a tutor next year.

THE JOURNALERS (descriptions provided by Meg)

Kate: Kate has an MFA from New Mexico State University and, in addition to teaching, is working on her first novel.

Jay: He's a new dad (he's married to Amy), will begin working toward an MFA at the New School in the Fall of 2001.

PRE-SESSION ORGANIZATION[4]

At the end of each academic year, Meg recruits two tutors—one long-term tutor (someone with more than one year of writing-center time) and one recently-hired tutor (someone with only one year of writing-center time)—who will work with her to plan that summer's weekly meetings. Together, they decide where to begin. Each year's planning sessions are a bit different, then, but they are all likely to involve re-reading articles from the previous year's meetings, reading new material, reading through staff journals, and brainstorming helpful activities. Meg writes that she has played around with the composition of this pre-session group, ensuring now, for example, that a recently-hired tutor always be part of the mix so that, for at least one person, "the questions and confusion of training and beginning to tutor are always fresh." Meg freely admits that she is tired of some of these readings, but her conversations with the tutors in the planning group remind her that "it's easy to forget what it's like when these issues are new to your life or when you get to name an experience for the first time." This summer the planning sessions featured, in addition to Meg, Jill as the recently-hired tutor and Mike (with two years of writing-center time) as the veteran tutor.

During their planning meetings, the three of them decided to drop the readings from the RIC Journal Book (a surprising decision, given the centrality of these journals, as I will take them up later) and to shift the focus of the readings. Mike points out that they "added a lot of new stuff" this year and that previous years' sessions had been more structured—"an issue per week." This year, they are trying to take what Mike calls "a holistic approach," using *Women's Ways of Knowing* as a base and arranging other essays around it. A goal of the planning group, as Meg described it to me, was to highlight a whole body/kinetic approach to education, one which "integrates experience and theory in order to move the group to a different level of understanding."

By the time I ask Mike and Jill to reflect in conversation with me about their experiences planning and executing (so to speak) the summer sessions, it has become clear that the tutors are resisting *Women's Ways*, and Jill, Mike, and Meg have reconsidered its place among the readings as a result. In response to my question about the biggest surprise of the summer, Mike leaps in with "scrapping half the curriculum, definitely." When I ask him how he feels about the fact that *Women's Ways* didn't work out as planned, he describes it as "the coolest thing that could've happened." Suspicious, I press him. "Why?" I ask. "Because it left some gaps open," he replies. In a jointly composed message to me, the three of them comment again on the scrapping of *Women's Ways*: "We felt that it was a wonderful failure . . . The three of us learned more about revision—in fact, what the summer syllabus doesn't show is the fact that it was revised almost weekly—and we rethought our emphasis."

Jill, for her part, is most surprised by the openness of the group. She deems them "more conversational" than last year's tutors, observing that "new people are participating more and more spontaneously." The whole session feels "not as planned or deliberate" to her as last year's sessions did. When I ask her why she thinks this might be, she offers that it might be because of a better ratio of old to new tutors, since last year she felt that the conversation was dominated by old tutors who "really seemed to know what they were talking about" and who, as a result, intimidated the new tutors. Mike supports her sense of the "vibe" in the Center and describes the room as "resonat[ing] from conversation," but Jill also admits that she feels "more relaxed" in the Writing Center now than she did when she first started, so her own comfort level may be influencing her reading of the interaction. In her final essay, Jill characterizes herself as "shy," and I was inclined to read her group interaction through this lens, until I re-read my notes from this interview, phrases and observations that made me think that Jill was quiet, in part, yes, because that is her way, but in part, too, by design, in an attempt to create space for others. I liked that.

The three of them, reading, writing, and talking together, giving shape to the summer's sessions. Reading through their messages to me, continuing our conversations, I so admire the work that Meg is doing: she has found a way to emphasize foundational principles of collaborative work and the political significance of literacy and education not only by way of the readings compiled to prepare tutors for this work, but also by inviting tutors into the design of their own and their peers' education in such significant ways.

Before the first meeting, each participant in the planning group writes a note to be included in the packet of materials.[5] Meg's is predictably teacher-like, though friendly and informal. Jill, in her role as representative new tutor, writes as a student to students: "Hi!" she begins. Though Meg's letter consisted of much housekeeping information—what students should have read and written, meeting times—Jill's letter contains none of that. Instead, she reflects on her newfound position relative to theirs ("It felt funny just then for me to be addressing you guys as 'new' when I'm so used to being one of the 'new' tutors. . . . There are no boundaries here between new and old. . . . We're all always learning together, and from each other. This summer will just be the beginning as we read theory together.") Jill explains the process of reading and re-reading: "Much of what we read is new to all of us, and some of us 'old' tutes [sic] will be revisiting theories, but even the old will be new again because all of you will be adding your thoughts and feelings about it. The ideas and concepts you bring in make it all different." Jill remarks that working in the writing center has been "a life changing experience," but she also promises that "we have fun here."

Mike, for his part, writes a poem to the new tutors. He echoes what Jill says, but also extends her comments by playing with them somewhat:

> the writing community that you have already entered
> will change as you write yourself into text
> the text writes your understanding of it
> in its letters and syntax
> the impacts of your questions will
> transform the norms
> that we think we hold dear,
> but collaborative discourse will persevere
> over the doctrines that we've already established
> we need your newness to embellish on
> the truth that is always failing to hold true.

In considering the impact of this succession of letters, I realize that my students only ever see the one that looks like Meg's. What have they missed if they don't see something like Jill's reflection on her development as a tutor, if they don't see Mike's language play, his challenge issued to them?

THE READINGS

A thick green binder sits at my feet, tabs marking off about every fifty pages or so. In it are copies of the selections that the RIC group read in preparation for each meeting. The binder is Meg's copy, and I brought it home with me because I thought it would help me tell the story, but it does not. In fact, it seems to work against the telling. The folder looks so uninhabited. And the presentation of readings—Week 1,

Week 2, Week 3—fails to account for the negotiation that went on between Jill, Mike, and Meg each week.

But, for what it's worth, here they are:

Meeting 1: June 19
Sondra Perl's "Understanding Composing"
Gail Godwin's "Rituals and Readiness: Getting Ready to
    Write"
Min-Zhan Lu's "From Silence to Words: Writing as Struggle"

Week 2: July 26
Beth Boquet's "'Our Little Secret': A History of Writing
    Centers, Pre-to Post-Open Admissions"
Kenneth Bruffee's "Collaborative Learning and the
    'Conversation of Mankind'"
Paolo Freire's *Pedagogy of the Oppressed*, Chapter 2

Week 3: July 3
Celebrate Independence Day—no meeting! no readings!

Week 4: July 10
Mike Rose's *Lives on the Boundary,* "Crossing Boundaries"
Mary Belenky et al., *Women's Ways of Knowing,* "Subjective
    Knowing"
Ilona Leki's *Understanding ESL Writers*, "Contrastive Rhetoric"

Week 5: July 17
Mary Belenky et al., *Women's Ways of Knowing,* "Procedural
    Knowing"
bell hooks's "Keeping Close to Home"

Week 6: July 24
Min-Zhan Lu's "Conflict and Struggle: The Enemies or
    Preconditions of Basic Writing?"
bell hooks's "'When I Was a Young Soldier for the Revolution':
    Coming to Voice"
Gloria Anzaldúa's "How to Tame a Wild Tongue"

Week 7: July 31
Jessica Benjamin's "First Bonds"

Nancy Welch's "Introduction," Chapter 1 ("Getting Restless"),
and Chapter 2 ("Collaborating with the Enemy")

Week 8: August 7
Kurt Spellmeyer's "After Theory: From Textuality to Attunement
with the World"
Mary Louise Pratt's "Arts of the Contact Zone"
Beth Boquet's "Channeling Jimi Hendrix, Or Ghosts in the
Feedback Machine"

DESCRIPTION OF THE RIC WRITING CENTER

Two days ago, in the midst of an email message to Michael
Spooner about book-related things, I signed off hurriedly when I
received word that someone from the Dean's office was coming to
take away our new computer—something about the Writing Center
having been reclassified as adjunct faculty office space and, as such, it
did not qualify for new equipment. (I won't even get started unpacking all the assumptions implicit in this last sentence.) When I
explained my log-out to Michael, he fired back, "Your *one* computer?" Yes, our one computer.

It occurred to me then, as it had occurred to me before, that we
make all sorts of assumptions about the spaces in which we operate. Our writing center at Fairfield is smaller and less well-
appointed than just about any I have ever seen (and yet it is bigger
and better-equipped than it was when I arrived). Others seem lav-
ish in comparison. Yet our writing center shares with other writing
centers many of the attributes we have come to expect: not only *a*
computer, but a coffee pot; not only MLA style manuals and
Random House dictionaries, but Polaroids of tutors past and present; not only an institutional paint job and adjustable book
shelves, but a couple of stained couches and a few plants in various
stages of distress.

It seems appropriate, in light of this acknowledgment, to offer
some description of the Writing Center at RIC, notes about what it
shares, probably, with most of the writing centers we're familiar
with, but also what is particular about it, because we all know

there's something particular about every one. So I asked the RIC tutors if they would tell me what seems important to say about their center to people who have never seen it. Here is a portion of Jill's response:

> It's December 8, and it's the first real snowfall of the season. Through the many windows of the WC, I can see buildings and grounds covered in white, students walking to and from class. The WC is very silent. Only the sound of a clicking computer keyboard and the scratch of my pencil can be heard. . . . After going to class all day in cold and impersonal spaces, the WC is a haven. Especially the backroom. The backroom is great. I've had so many great con-versations there with everyone. The couches and chairs . . . are comfy. The lamp is great. Just getting away from harsh fluorescent lighting for a while helps your mood. . . . The big windows I've stared out for hours and just thought, or better yet didn't think at all. . . . The bulletin board with flyers, pictures of tutors old and new at conferences, weddings. Cards, drawings, momentos—all of these things remind me that I'm not alone.

Jill writes more than a solid page about what she calls the "back-room," a converted closet in the back of the Writing Center where tutors tend to hang out when they're not officially "on." I find it fascinating, though not surprising, that Jill's description of the Writing Center begins with a consideration of the ways in which she finds both comfort (which we might easily associate with writing centers) and solitude (which we might be less likely to associate with writing centers) in that backroom. She is a page and a half into her response before she begins to describe what she calls "the WC itself," and she positions that writing center *in relation to* the backroom:

> Outside the backroom, there is the WC itself. It's bright and open, with large windows across one wall. Food greets people when they enter.

As I read Jill's response, I am glad that I didn't try to write this description on my own, as observer rather than inhabitant of this writing center, because the aspects she chose to foreground are not ones that were immediately apparent to me, and the objects that make up the background (or at least the tail-end of a lengthy single-spaced email message) are the ones that would have been most likely to gain my attention:

> The decorations are fun too. It makes the atmosphere more fun and lively. Every holiday, practically, we decorate. . . .The decorations are also a conversation starter when someone comes in all stressed out. There are certainly enough conversation pieces here. The giant Scream doll, posters by various artists, puppets, toys, markers, paper. It's almost like elementary school for big kids. Lots of colors and textures everywhere.

I love the image of the writing center as an "elementary school for big kids," an image that instantly calls up the activities of the summer session (which I will cover later in this chapter).

Mike sent his email message from London, where he spent the fall semester studying. The Writing Center is no doubt less colorful, less textured, for his absence, but his distance provides an interesting perspective. Rather than sitting in the Writing Center composing his description, as I imagine Jill might have done, or even composing it from home, having just spent the afternoon working there, Mike crafts his response from a flat somewhere in England. He begins by offering a concession to what might be an "appropriate" response:

> it could be summed up in the plaster rectangle with artsy posters and a coffee pot tucked in the left wing of a modernist craig lee [the name of the building] asbestos hut . . . we do have posters and pictures . . . and food . . . the aim of a free environment.

From here, he takes off, describing the Writing Center as it exists for him in his time and his place, now.

our conversations have taken us out of that physical place
and into the space that the actual dialogue happens
. . . if you want my most true, recent description, it would have
to be the wide boulevard-style stairwell with sparse blue carpet
and resonant steel railings, talking to a smiling belgian girl
about fate being the moving force that is me . . . inside me . . .
how this relates to literary analysis . . . through flemish to
english . . . or the doppleganager themes in poe and gogel in
the small rectangle dorm room with crude fluorescent long
bulbs and speeding traffic through the small ventalation [sic]
window facing new cross high street . . . or the kitchen in
loring hall flat A 6, speaking to claudine . . . a confident british
student completely frustrated with her stuffy professorial-type
professor for belittling her unconstructively about the shape of
her latin american colonial economics paper . . . she found
that just talking out loud about it made her ideas come out that
she didn't get a chance to do on her own . . . . the
writing center is wide and long, stretching everywhere the conversation will take it . . . expanding to immense girth without
wearing out . . . it is the discourse . . .
    this is the RIC writing center I know at this point.

THE SUMMER MEETINGS

    Meetings began at 4:30 P.M., and tutors trickled in beginning at
around 4:00. Mike and Jill were around all afternoon, since the
2:00–4:00 P.M. hours were their scheduled tutoring slots on Mondays
in the summer. Others came in after classes or from work or from
home. Occasionally people would arrive early and settle into the
backroom to finish reading one of the day's selections or to write a
response. By 4:15, anyone around was drafted into furniture arrange-
ment, setting up tables and chairs in a manner that would facilitate
conversation and dinner. The six small tables in the Writing Center
are shaped like trapezoids, so most days we simply fit the puzzle
pieces together and put the food in the middle—bagels, hummus,
chicken and tuna salads, grapes.

Meeting 1: Monday, June 26

Meeting 1, like the first meeting of any class, was tentative. The new tutors (especially Lisa and Justin) eyed the place nervously and waited for cues from the others, particularly with regards to the food, following the lead of the old tutors, who dove into the bagels with gusto just as the meeting got underway. Bryan settled in a bit more easily and seemed bemused by the interactions. The new folks hesitated when discussing the readings, but Meg, Mike, and Jill trudged forward gamely. The video of the meeting reveals an empty chair between Bryan and Justin behind which stands a life-sized blow-up version of Munch's *The Scream.* As the camera pans, *The Scream* appears to be part of the group, expressing what Lisa and Justin might be thinking at right about this time. Interestingly, throughout the course of the summer, there is only one occasion in which anyone chooses to sit in front of *The Scream;* so, given the poor depth perception of the video camera (or of my tired eyes), the character seems to be part of the interaction. Indeed, as new tutors engage more and more in the life of the summer sessions, *The Scream* too becomes increasingly integrated into the group, even getting dressed up as part of a performative piece at a later summer meeting.

Watching the video of this first meeting, Meg and I decide that we both talked too much during the first hour. It was teacherly: "Let's discuss the readings you were assigned for today." The students responded dutifully, looking down when a question was posed, offering brief responses when pressed or when the wait became embarrassingly long. It was not until the end of the meeting, when Mike proposed a story game we've come to call "Pass the Beast," that people began to loosen up. Mike explained the activity as follows: "I'll start the story game by saying a few words. Then I'll throw The Beast [a stuffed armadillo-type rag animal]. If I throw The Beast to you, then you, umm, have to say a few words and throw it to somebody else." Nervous smiles and laughter from the group as people look around. There's some discussion regarding how best to facilitate the interaction and finally people stand—some on the ground, a few (Meg, Sarah, and Mike) on chairs. Mike begins:

"Billy the Beetle received no pasta on Tuesday."

He pitches The Beast to Sarah, who continues: "Because on Tuesday pasta is illegal in Saskatchewan."

Sarah pitches it to Lisa, who emits a long, tortured "ummmm" followed by more nervous laughter. At this point, Lisa receives some coaching from the group: "Just say anything." "Anything is fine." She just keeps saying "ummmm" and finally simply hands it to Justin, who is standing anxiously to her right. Justin passes The Beast from one hand to another. More "ummmms" followed by a "Can we start over?" and an admission: "I'm not creative." He continues passing The Beast back and forth between his own two hands while the others prompt him, as they had prompted Lisa, by reminding him that he can say *anything*. Finally, he takes them literally and re-asserts his "I'm not creative" statement as his contribution to the storyline, at which point he throws The Beast to Bryan, who looks surprised and then offers: "Life in the forest was good." And the story is off and running.

The story begins to move faster and faster, and the old tutors model what a person can do when she is stuck with The Beast, can think of nothing to say, and just wants to get rid of it *fast*. Adding on is a favorite tactic in such cases. Amy models an "and more peas" phrase, which is all she tacked on to a list of things that the beast might eat. Lisa catches on to this by the next time The Beast comes to her:

Mike: The beetle said, "Have some more pasta."
Joanne: The dog gave it to Peter.
Lisa: Who gave it to Jill.

Lisa is visibly excited by her clever contribution, and the others are too. Everyone implicitly recognizes that Lisa has caught on, and the next time The Beast comes to her, she is bold enough to shift the storyline a bit by introducing suspense: "But then the armadillos stepped up." She pitches The Beast and, after passing through a few more hands, it is returned to Bryan, who takes the action to its climactic moment: "By this time the people of Saskatchewan had had it."

The story goes on for a few more rounds until Sarah declares:

The people of Saskatchewan paved paradise and put up a parking lot.

She tosses The Beast to Meg, who deems this "The End" as several people start singing the Joni Mitchell song "Big Yellow Taxi" and explaining, to those who are mildly confused, that this was the referent for Sarah's conclusion. The tape at this point is obscured by laughter and by the numerous discussions splintering off among participants as people resume their seats.

Contrasting this activity to some of the more typical icebreaker activities, I ask the tutors why Pass-The-Beast seemed more appropriate in terms of their own preparation. Sarah was quick to offer a response. She first characterized more typical greet-the-student advice as "reductive." The story game, she explained, "preserves the complexity of the interaction. It puts people on the spot but it also allows you to support them. You have to really pay attention to what other people have said. You have to think about the people who are coming after you. You have to think about what role you as a participant are playing in the game at that particular moment."

Meeting 2: Monday, June 26

Meeting 1 was *supposed* to wrap up with a mapping activity, where tutors would map the story of The Beast that they had just created. The story ended up being too chaotic (and too long) to try to map, so that activity was abandoned and the meeting was effectively adjourned. At the beginning of the second meeting, then, Meg revisits the issue of mapping as a technique and divides the tutors into teams of two or three to map out the day's readings. The tutors get colorful markers and large white pads as they sit cross-legged on the floor of the Writing Center, circling the area to find a favorite spot. Upon reviewing the tape of this meeting, Meg declares that this activity "didn't work as well" as some of the others did. "It's traditional," she observes, "an academic project." She's right, and though we see a few interesting moments—what Mike does with color, how Bryan uses solid lines and dotted lines—we also notice that the tutors' texts are never far from them, literally or figuratively. Justin, for instance, repeatedly flips back to see what he has highlighted that might need to be transcribed onto the paper. Joanne and Donna produce a wonderfully chaotic, messy map that Joanne promptly crumples up once she has copied it over into a neat pyramid. Donna sits back and watches her.

In a later conversation, I ask Mike whether he recommends strategies to other students that he himself does not use. He explains that he is always seeking "multiple channels," other ways in. He sees it as crucial that tutors stretch and elasticize their own processes. At the same time, he acknowledges that there are activities that just don't seem to work for him and that he "almost never" uses in a tutoring session. Mapping is one of them. I am surprised, then, that the tutors chose to use it as the central activity for this second meeting of the summer. I talk to Mike about my own experiences teaching, about my pedagogical Believing-Game maxim: if you believe it, they will do it. But if you don't believe it, if it doesn't engage you—as tutor, as teacher—then you're all dead in the water.

Conversation is the word most frequently used by the tutors to describe all of their activities: the summer meetings, the journals, tutoring sessions, their relationship with each other and with Meg. So it should not be surprising that our conversation—Mike's and mine—turned to a consideration of the responsibilities of the students in these interactions. Mike talks about his recent experiences with Jason, a Korean student who "comes in with nothing." His goal is to read, write, and speak more English. "So," Mike says, "in the beginning there's this constant pressure of like 'What do we do? What do we do?' So we do drawings and freewrites to try to open up the process for both of us, just symbols and diagrams and then we write and talk about them." I ask him what they talk about. "Just plain old talking. Where we both are, as people. We use visual imagery to supplement conversation. As a kind of relay." Mike shows me a specific example of drawings and writing they did the previous week. They began by tracing out their hands. Mike's is relaxed and open. Jason's, while not quite curled into a fist, is tense. Jason freewrites around the perimeter of the drawing, listing the things his hand can do: the fingers can pinch, can lift, can squeeze. From here he writes about his habit of clutching a golf ball in his hand

and squeezing it when he is anxious. He says that last year at this time, his golf ball was his constant companion because he was sad and depressed, but now he has less need for it. He feels better.

Mike describes these sessions with Jason as mutually satisfying because Jason is so willing to enter into the work. For their next meeting, Jason is bringing one of his golf balls and, Mike says, "We'll see what we can do with it."

Meetings 3 and 4: Monday, July 10 and Monday, July 17

The third meeting marks the start of more intense wrestling with texts and more extended discussions between the tutors, with less intervention from Meg. At this meeting, the tutors begin to discuss *Women's Ways of Knowing*. At the same time, the new tutors have figured out that these texts are intended to be provocative, not categorically accepted by the group. Bryan commented to Meg, for example, that he hadn't realized that they were going to be *encouraged* to disagree with the material presented to them. He seems relieved and freed by this discovery.

What's revealed on this tape (and what becomes more evident in Meeting 4) are the ways in which students work through a difficult text together. The tasks require the tutors to struggle in much the same way that writing center students struggle with assignments, texts, and ideas. The tutors in this meeting, then, rather than consider explicitly *how* to work with a student who has a difficult text, find themselves engaged in the same project as the students with whom they will eventually work. Several of the tutors observe, for example, that they had never encountered such diverse and challenging readings prior to their first summer session.[6] In an interview, Jill characterizes her "view of people and of the world [as] much more limited" before she began tutoring. The combination of the readings, the conversation about the readings, and the environment in which it all took place has given her more confidence in herself. At the same time, these activities have left her "more open-minded to other people and ideas, to how other people think." When considering *Women's Ways of Knowing* during this particular meeting, the tutors comment on *how* they read it: they talk about

where Belenky et al. rely on theory; they discuss the role the anec-
dotes play in the text; they remark on the nature of a qualitative
study.

The previous sentence masks the complexity of the scene, of
course. In general, the process is often unsettling, especially to the
new tutors. In follow-up interviews, nearly everyone admitted that
they felt a bit off balance during their first summer session. On the
tape at this point, Meg and I see evidence of this as Justin alternately
sits forward and then back, engaging and disengaging, sometimes
scratching his forehead with his pen. The old tutors must also expect
to be caught off guard (if one can ever expect such a thing), reminding themselves to be open to hearing new interpretations of material
they may think they know inside and out. (This is how they ended up
revising the emphasis of the summer session midway through the
course.) The dense passages require unpacking, connecting as peers,
finding multiple ways into the text. The tutors connect it to other
pieces they've read, either as a group or individually, readings that
were easier for them, that made more sense. They, quite frankly, tutor
each other until some temporary closure is reached.

By the end of the meeting, the tutors have moved away from the
Belenky text and are talking about Rose's portrayal of education.
Mike says, "We conceptualize art differently than we conceptualize
schooling—it's like remediation. It's like, you're not working toward
anything creative. You're just working toward this linear method of
thought. I mean, to get any sort of praise outside of that, you have to
break that. It's like, go inside that cage I made for you, and I'll be
impressed when you break out." [Laughter erupts.] Bryan adds,
"Yeah, like, you must be some sort of mutation—how'd you get out?"
Mike continues, "It's like, 'Oh, I guess you're cool enough to have a
beer with,' you know."

A pretty stinging indictment, especially if you've ever shared a beer
with a student.

Meeting 4 has the group returning to *Women's Ways of Knowing*.
People have openly admitted that they dislike the text; they character-
ize it as "reductive" (Bryan) and claim that it has "an elitist air to it"
(Donna) when compared to hooks's piece that the group has also

read for this week. Nonetheless, the tutors do give it a generous reading. For example, when one person raises an objection, another person will frequently attempt to rescue the text. Bryan, for instance, criticizes the authors for studying down: "Let's look at these people who didn't have all the advantages we had." In response, Justin, who has his share of problems with the text, contrasts the *Women's Ways of Knowing* group with the wealthy, elite group that Perry chose to focus on, making the point that we might not otherwise have heard those voices at all.

Meeting 4 ends with a very specific return to the texts, but an interesting one, as tutors spontaneously begin their own read-around, reading together their favorite quotes from hooks's essay, a piece they all seemed to like. Donna, Bryan, Mike, Meg, and Jill all offer their favorite passages while the others testify softly in the background—"Oh, yeah," "Oh, I like that one," "Yeah, yeah"—with each flip of a page.

Reflecting on meetings like these, Sarah admits that, as a beginning tutor, "all this theory doesn't feel like a wealth of information. It feels like we just talked all summer, like a whole bunch of ideas." In retrospect, though, she says she is glad that there was no handbook or template on tutoring to follow: "If I had had that, I would have felt secure. The summer sessions taught me that you have to be invested, have to hear them, have to hear what they need from you, what you can offer them. It gives you a lot of freedom."

For Mike, the summer sessions create "enforced equal confusion," or critical unease, that leads each participant in the group to consider where-am-I and to ask, how does another person go through this process? He sees parallels with the students who come to the RIC Writing Center because "that's where students are when they come here." The best sessions, according to Mike, occur when both participants—tutor and student—are involved in a "mutual creation process." The worst sessions, when a tutor says, oh, I've been through this. The result: "Blocks happen because you're not creating; you're just spouting out." In general, Mike says, the summer sessions prepared him for tutoring by inducing a state of "relaxed readiness, of constant tension and release, flexing and stretching."

Meeting 5: Monday, July 24

By this time, the pre-session discussions have become increasingly lively, and this fifth meeting marks a real turning point.

The meeting begins with an activity. Meg declares that the group will be engaged in "a different kind of composing." As she talks, Mike gathers markers, pens, pencils and paper and distributes them across the tables. Meg continues, "By drawing, indicate to people who you are. Or, take what you know about your own culture and make a composite." She explains that drawing is just "another way in." Predictably, she gets questions of clarification. "We draw?" asks Bryan. "You draw," replies Meg.

Again, the old tutors take the lead. Joanne pulls the caps off a set of markers: "Oh, these are the scented ones." They begin passing markers back and forth across the table. Somehow, a whole bunch of the markers have wound up in front of Jill, and when Joanne requests one, Jill jokes, "I failed sharing."

As Barbara, our videographer, pans the group, we see Mike and Donna already deep in concentration. Mike is making concentric circles with a pencil. Jill and Joanne take longer to get into it and are still a little chatty at the other end of the table. Lisa and Justin have not yet started to draw and are looking off into the distance for inspiration, Lisa with her hands clasped together near her mouth, elbows on the table.

Every few minutes, someone touches base about what's supposed to be going on, and different group members respond to the questions. At one point, for example, Donna asks, "So this is about me?" Mike, who is sitting next to her, responds, "Yeah. Your essence." "My essence?" Donna replies querulously. Mike, without looking up from his circles, "Yeah, captures your essence."

Barbara turns the camera back on Mike, who is now drawing lines radiating out from the center of his circles. We can actually *hear* Mike drawing, even when the camera is not filming him. His pace becomes frantic. Even looking down to take notes, I can tell whether he's drawing circles or lines or squiggles. It's rhythmic and hypnotic.

As the activity draws to a close, people begin commenting on each other's drawings and offering brief explanations of their own. Mike has to be stopped (by Meg).

Donna offers to show hers first. It is an arresting sketch, pencil on white paper, of her body on the face of a clock. Very spare. She begins,

> I'm standing on my head. Well, actually, I'm standing on one hand. My kids are in my [other] palm, and at my feet [which are up in the air] I have a pile of books for school and on the other [foot] I have my computer, and all these things demand my time. I'm on the clock because time is a thing that really kinda weighs on me, like I don't have a lot of time, like my kids are growing and that's time, and things that I have to do take up time, and time is running out, and I'm kinda like the hands of the clock because of how I use my time is what's important, you know what I mean? And a lot of this [page] is empty because I don't feel like, while I have to do all this stuff . . . Politically speaking I'm like a fringe person because of the lifestyle choices that I've made and because of politics and the place that I occupy in our society because my husband passed away and because me and my kids fit between the cracks and I fall between the cracks income-wise so it's kinda difficult to exist financially and otherwise, so . . .

Her voice trails off. People are quiet. Mike offers a soft "awesome" and nods his head. Bryan says, "Cool." Donna puts her sketch down on the table.

Bryan's rendering is fascinating, too, and he begins his explanation by stating plainly, "This is me." He goes on:

> It is a world of swirling ego and hierarchy. What I have is, uhhh, the see-through pyramid. It has the disconnected eye at the top, symbolizing awareness of my own ego construct, which is just a bunch of me's on top of me. And then I have the guy in the middle who's looking at both in disbelief and it's got the reverse image of the eye trying to be aware of

what the hell's going on, but it's kinda hard. And there's [points to a stick figure walking toward a clump of trees] my hopeful aspirations just to leave it all behind and travel, you know, not in a bad way but just like, you know, no more hierarchies, no more nothing, just off in the woods.

And then there's Mike, who holds up what used to be a large white page, now covered with graphite:

I was working just like with circles, just the idea of circles and it's, like, with the interconnections of everything so in essence I am the process of circles, the process where orbits and ellipses make solid black out of graphite, out of constant lines. It's like trying to draw through music, no longer visual representations but just drawing as music, like with rhythms and trying different rhythm strokes and stuff like that and then things come out cyclically and form more multiple infinite more circles and coming out of infinite centers. One of the things that's really cool about it is starting out with basic patterns like concentric circles or swirls then going with lines or degrees that shoot out and then every time I do it I progress and I get bored with that and then I do something different and then I'll do like wavy lines shooting out or the same lines start turning into circles or stuff like that. So it's trying to get at ideas of the infinite essence that we're all intertwined with . . .

He then pulls out a second page.

The other cool part I like is this as the tandem piece to it, which is where it breaks out totally on itself and I couldn't do what I wanted to do on this [the first] sheet of paper and it has to break out.

Once everyone's drawings had been presented, there was no further formal discussion of them. Meg admitted to me later that she believed that was a missed opportunity. Perhaps. But the work that followed the presentations was so rich, it's hard to imagine a better opportunity, and I am certain that the groundwork laid by their artistic efforts played an important role in the discussions that followed.

Jill began, shortly after Mike wrapped up his description of his piece/s, by referring to my Hendrix chapter, which the tutors were reading in draft form. She said, "It seems like creativity is born out of confusion." And then she observed that this was "not something our school systems teach. Everything's supposed to be clear-cut. You're not supposed to be confused by things. I know I think that way a lot, like, 'I'm not supposed to be confused by this.'"

Donna agrees, "It does lay a foundation with lots of cracks. . . . It makes people mental." When others laugh, she laughs too, but then she looks down at her paper, raises her eyebrows, and reiterates, "It does."

Discussion turns to the second essay by hooks and veers to a place some might consider far off-task—to the Arab-Israeli conflict and to questions of land ownership. Before weighing in with her opinion on this topic, Donna clears this with Meg: "Is this an appropriate . . . you know." Meg replies, "Nothing is inappropriate." Donna says, "OK." The discussion continues for a while. Mike brings the discussion back around just a bit by saying, "All this stuff is asking us to get rid of our hierarchical thinking . . . I think we just need to go to ground zero." Bryan responds, "I think it's essential to be aware of as many things as possible." Donna tries to interrupt—"But since that's not gonna happen . . . " She's talked over a couple of times before she finally gets to make her point:

Since that's not gonna happen, how do you work within the boundary that you have? If people don't talk about stuff, you need to keep bringing it up until the pain is at a manageable point, right, so everybody can deal, cuz that's what it's all about, right? It's all about pain, basically. It's all about fights and wars and feeling oppressed and not having any freedom so the bottom line is when you're oppressed and you have no freedom and you can't learn and you can't do stuff, then you're in pain and then you act bad . . . .People need to maintain their integrity. You need to lift people up out

of the cracks through, what?, education, right? . . . So that's
what we've been reading.

Justin jumps in here. "Are people in that much pain? I mean, is it
really that bad?" he asks. "Everybody's doing pretty well, I think," he continues. "I mean, everybody here's doing well." Throughout his observation, Donna shakes her head across the table and mutters, increasingly
loudly, "No, no, no, no." When Justin finishes, Donna continues,

> The word pain—it's just part of the picture. I think labels
> like "good" or "bad" . . . defeat what's going on . . . . I think it
> just *is*. Like, I fight every day. I have to come here every day. I
> live on a really tiny amount of money. My place in the
> political structure of this country—I'm a very marginalized
> woman, you know. Things could be better for me.

The back-and-forth is frank and raw as people openly disagree,
and say so. At this point, (with the possible exception of Justin) most
seem to agree that revolution is necessary, but what constitutes revolution, or how a revolution might take place, is up for grabs. Here's
Donna again:

> Frankly, if you're living on $50 a week and you don't even
> have anything in your fridge and you have nothing for your
> kids, where you gonna get the strength, if you can't even eat,
> to do that [the cultural work of revolution]? You're not. Cuz
> you're dying. Emotionally, psychologically, physically. You're
> dying a really slow, horrible death. It's a terrible thing.

This is not an academic issue for Donna. The situation she just
described is her own.

> *Bryan:* It's a really effective way of controlling people.
> *Donna:* Yeah. And that's why we have to help people.
> When you write, it's so personal. It's like channeling your
> innermost thing, even if it's a totally fluff thing. It's still a
> really personal thing, any word that comes out of your
> fingers.

From here a discussion ensues about maintaining the integrity of writing and of the writer. That topic comes back around to Donna, who finishes it up this way:

I think . . . that there is a way . . . to express yourself so that it expresses *you* on paper and that you can polish it so that it will get you the B or the A in the classroom. From my own personal experience, I'm a very idiosyncratic person and I have a very idiosyncratic way of writing and it works for me because I take the cues which I've kept and I can put the paper out and I think that that is a skill that we can give to people who come here. I think that it is possible. Which is one reason that I'm here. People can come here with their personal experiences, their cultural lives, and it can be accepted . . . without the person losing their integrity.

Then, in the next moment, she completely shifts gears, turns her body toward Meg, and asks,

What if you get a person who just can't put a sentence together? What do you do? Do you just . . . *teach* them?

At the end of this evening's session, Mike proposes a round-robin improv music event:

We could go through this [what we've been doing] in some musical way. Like, we have musical instruments in front of us, all around us [referring to all the objects on the table]. I'll start a basic pattern or rhythm, and anyone, we can just slowly just start picking up, it doesn't have to be in order either but just as you start feeling something just add anything, any noise, any movement, any rhythm. Feel free to elaborate, change. OK.

Mike takes a deep breath, closes his eyes, and begins by slapping a 4/4 beat with his bare hands on his chest. This elicits an exchange of knowing smiles from Bryan and Jill. Meg starts popping the table with her hands, and Jenn picks up a ring of keys and begins shaking them in syncopation. Jenn's act is the defining moment of the jam; she vibrates in sympathy with Mike. The others feel the vibration, too, and they start to find the gaps, find a way in, enter the groove. Justin clicks the top of his pen. Bryan takes a pen and runs it along the corrugated side of a Poland Spring water bottle. Mike shifts gears once a critical mass is reached, drumming on a container of Skippy peanut butter instead of his chest. Slowly, the session winds down. Everyone falls off except Mike, who continues the beat, in 4/4 rhythm, for one final measure.

Meeting 6: Monday, July 31

The post-break segment of Meeting 6 takes up an earlier, but brief, discussion of the selections from Nancy Welch's book. All the building materials are brought to the table—legos, toobers and zots, markers, toys—and Meg asks the tutors to "think about representing what death-work and life-work might be for you. A drawing or a conversation or build death-work. Try to see if you can somehow represent it."

Barbara focuses the camera on Mike and follows him through his entire process. I can see why: He *is* fascinating to watch. He begins by returning to his circles and lines, this time on two pieces of big, bright yellow posterboard. He crumples them up, one inside the other, and punches his fists through them. He is now wearing the posters like giant, golden handcuffs. Eventually, he pulls his hands out of them, positions them on the table, and starts clipping at the crumpled edges with scissors. Next, he applies pieces of tape at seemingly random junctures. Finally, he drizzles glue all over it. Not surprisingly, his piece has drawn a lot of attention by the end of the activity, and Mike is the first one to offer an explanation of his life-/death-work:

> I wanted to take the piece that I had been working on [from last week's activity] so that it would be a real revision— screw that—I ripped it up—so I started to apply life-work to it by bringing it back together, stitching it, taping it, so it just looks really weird now. [He regards it momentarily.] It's just dripping and it smells. It's basically a mess.

The piece begins to settle as Mike is talking. Meg jokes, "It's still creating itself." Mike finishes,

I think this is one of the best revision processes I've ever done. It's opened up the process a lot.

At the other end of the room, *The Scream*, which Meg has decorated as part of her depiction of death-work, collapses under the weight of the umbrella she added. Mike calls it "a performance piece."

Next, Amy holds up an 8½ x 11-inch piece of computer paper on which she has sketched, in pencil, "the death-work tree." It is striated, like ligature, and looks like a skinned human hand. Amy begins simply:

I like trees. I have nothing to grab onto. I have to like shimmy up the tree and sometimes that's really easy and sometimes it's really hard and then once I get there there are all these different places I can go to and I come this way and its difficult to make myself come all the way out here and so OK now I have to come back down here and go over there and explore these parts and sometimes the branches might not hold me and then I might fall to the ground and have to start all over again and even if I could explore all the branches by the time I was done new branches might have grown.

She's done explaining, but she continues to hold up the tree for a moment before putting it down and turning her attention to Lisa.

Lisa remarks that she had "about a thousand different things going through [her] head so this is open to any interpretation." Using toobers and zots, she has constructed an abstract piece that is difficult to describe. Its basic properties consist of a stable axis on which other objects rotate. The rotating objects on each side of the axis are identical, so the piece is balanced in that way. The object in the middle is the only one of its kind. Even if you can't imagine the piece, I think you can appreciate her explanation:

Well, it could be two separate people and, in order for communication to occur, it has to go through this barrier [the one-of-a-kind object in the middle] and the barrier is the one part of this piece—it's symmetrical, it's organized, and it's not about to fall apart—but it's hindering communication. All these things [the objects at either end of the axis] represent the ideas and the beliefs they're trying to communicate to each other and in order to do that they first have to pass through the barrier. And to look at it as far as revision [another possible interpretation], this could be where you are [indicates one side of the axis], this could be where you're trying to get [indicates the other side].

When she's finished explaining, I observe, "The way you talked about it, the barrier is the only thing that's not contingent." Mike, picking up on a part of my own representation of death-work, offers a quote from Davis: "What it shares is sharing itself."

The Final Meeting

In her notes for the first meeting, Meg has a "reminder" to be shared with the tutors: "By the end of the summer, each person will be responsible for a piece of writing that explores one or more of the readings in more detail." Periodically throughout the summer, Meg brings up the topic of the essay, asking people how much they have written (which very quickly, as we might expect, turns into a question of whether or not they have *anything* written). Tutors, as we all probably know, are as likely as any other student to procrastinate, to start and re-start a paper incessantly, particularly since tutors often feel a great deal of pressure, especially initially, to demonstrate their skill at writing. These difficulties are compounded, during the RIC summer session, by some of the other pressing issues in the tutors' lives—work for their credit-bearing courses, for example, or just plain life issues like the ones that have already been transcribed. By the July 17th meeting, Meg's reminder reads, in all caps:

THINK ABOUT THE PAPER YOU'LL BE WRITING FOR OUR LAST SESSION. BRING SOMETHING IN WRITING TO SHARE WITH AT LEAST ONE OTHER PERSON DURING THE MEETING.

Meg's something-in-writing is evidence of her frustration at the tutors' willingness to talk about thoughts that they had regarding their papers but their unwillingness to commit anything to the actual page.

All tutors—old and new—were expected to contribute their own essays, and the final meeting was reserved for people to read their papers aloud and for others to comment on them individually. I was pleasantly surprised by their papers, which, for the most part, turned out to read less like essays for a class than like precursors to the kinds of explorations the tutors are expected to do in the journal. They didn't reference the readings nearly as much nor as formally as I had expected, even though it was clear that they had all read them. And the papers were achingly personal.

The meeting that evening began with Meg reading Jill's paper aloud. (Though Jill had to miss the last meeting, she sent her essay along so that Meg could read it to us.) At the top of the essay, where the title would normally be, is instead an epigraph from Freire about the problem of the "banking model" of education. Jill's first paragraph describes the relevance of this quote:

> I've been struggling with writing this, and I just figured out
> why. I want to describe to you the impact working here has
> had on the way I think, and I just realized that I can't do that
> without describing to you the way I used to think, and why. I
> was trying to write words that would be "detached from reality,
> disconnected from the totality that engendered them . . . " [the
> reader is to understand that Jill has lifted these phrases from the
> Freire quote], so I wouldn't have to open myself up. I was
> doing what I've told students in tutoring sessions not to do,
> going against every theory I've read here over the past year. I
> was going to try and write this without making a connection
> between my personal life and how theory has changed me,
> when I realized this is impossible to do.

Jill's next paragraph begins with this declaration: "I have always wished that I was not so shy." After describing the sort of person she is not—one who "can make small talk with anyone, say hello to perfect strangers"—Jill admits to being able to "identify with many of the women in *Women's Ways of Knowing*," and she offers another block quote here, part of which reads, "Growing up without opportunities for play and for dialogue poses the gravest danger for the growing child." She acknowledges, in her analysis following this quote, that for much of her life she "didn't think to speak at all" and then attributes her shyness to "the way [she] grew up."

> I grew up living with just my mother, my parents divorcing when I was six. Since it was just us, I spent a lot of time amusing myself, either reading or being outside. I was alone often, so I really had no reason to speak aloud. My mother also suffers from mental illness. She has obsessive compulsive disorder (OCD), agoraphobia, and depression. OCD can manifest itself in many ways, and her way was in organizing and cleaning house. Needless to say, I lived in a very controlled and stifling environment. I was afraid to move in that house, because if I messed anything up, she would get mad at me. As I grew older, I realized that the way we lived was very different from other people, and this also contributed to my silence. I felt very different from everyone else.

In the next paragraph, Jill analyzes in more detail the impact of this environment on her life outside of her home, particularly on her school routine:

> The more aware of my silence I became, the more quiet I was. I would sit there in class or when just hanging around with friends and think to myself "I should be saying something, what can I say that will be interesting enough?" I didn't think anything I had to say was important enough to say aloud. I didn't realize that people say anything, whether it's important or not.

(I love this last realization. I smile every time I read it.)

The last third of Jill's paper considers the impact of her work in the writing center on her own personal development:

The way I think is so different now than it was two years ago, and much of it has to do with the writing center, and the theory we have read. Working here has helped draw me out of myself. . . . The readings we have read here have opened my eyes to the world. I was so inside myself, so introverted, so focused on myself, that I was not letting anything else in. I was going through the motions with everything, I knew how to do school, but I wasn't really trying to learn anything, nor was I questioning whether I really was learning anything.

Here she inserts another quote from Freire, this one about critical consciousness, which, Jill claims, is "what [she] has developed working here," and she concludes with two beautiful, revealing statements:

I feel like I am actually participating in life rather than just watching it like a film.

[This new way of thinking] allows me to see myself as a part of the whole world, instead of being alone inside my own world.

Through most of the summer, Jill had provided a stark, and necessary, contrast to Mike's presentation of self, and their papers offer much the same sorts of distinctions.

Mike's introduction reads, "at the piano/cooling, composing long landscapes of innuendo./in everything,/the music opening, laughing at my hands and the keys in labour[.]" Mike is one of the tutors who started and restarted his paper on an almost weekly basis, and in his first paragraph, he explains what he's been working toward:

what i'm trying to put my finger on is the theory or life rhythm that all my actions flow through, regardless of social or physical context. i want to connect the theory of the writing center, something i consider a beautiful practice of reciprocity, to the breathing network of cultures and symbols that we encounter in our other sphere of existence . . . in essence, to explain how what happens here at our center is in harmony and critical counterpoint to the formless source of all biologic music that we are attuned to.

Mike is a self-taught musician who routinely adjourns to the campus practice rooms to jam on the pianos, and he is part of a hip-hop freestyling community, a practice that informs most of the writing of his essay. He tells the story, for example, of a late-night conversation at the beach with his friend Ryan, who feels intimidated by the skill of the other freestylers in their group, including Mike. They walk along, and Mike writes:

> silence, save for ocean threats two waves deep. every time i tried to flow with ryan, rather than encourage him it only stifled him. when i let my process, my rhythm flow free in the night sky, it only composed shovels for ryan's mind to bury itself with. so this is my beautiful creative process. my connection to my self and my desire to express my emotions and mind patterns to my friends only ends in silencing them.

In the next paragraph, then, Mike wonders,

> if i could describe the beauty that i feel, the "attunement" [referring to the spellmeyer piece] to the world around me through rhythm, the joy of expirementation [sic] as, say, a coming to voice—then what impacts [sic] does this coming to voice have upon me, and how will this freedom i feel be interpreted by others around me?

This question leads Mike into another narrative, one where he feels moved to flow in front of a group of his friends by a magnificent Fourth of July fireworks display. He then has to consider the effects of this demonstration:

> morgan is an acquaintance who i don't particularly enjoy the presence of. on recent occasions he has expressed racist ideas that turn me away from his energy. he is smug and arrogant, and wears the prejudices of his parenting proudly . . . the night after the firework display . . . morgan started freestyling to me . . . unexpectedly . . . i could see the

excitement in his eyes, the liquid rhythm flowing through him
. . . he told me this was his first time flowing in public, that
my display at the fireworks the previous night had inspired
him to begin his journey into new voice. this scared me, in
fact i was horrified.

To explain his dismay at this prospect, Mike describes what he sees as
the purpose of flow:

flowing allows for improvisational critique and question,
calling attention to all social mores and patterns of logic and
communication . . . flow is an art of living so perfectly in the
present tense. i feared the stability of morgan as a conduit of
the flow . . . from his racist comments and arrogance, he
could use the force of inifinite poetry towards means of
oppression, inspiring fear, exclusion—he now had a platform
for speaking, i was very worried of his campaigning.
    had i created a monster?

Mike's solution to Morgan's presentation was to respond in kind:

in flow, in a response to his call, i layed down basic rules
of righteousness to adhere to in flow . . . how to be sensitive
to the silences and pauses of others, how to understand the
mutual growing process of everyone involved, how to always
channel the flow in positivity . . . i directly addressed him . . .
telling him to be free of all prejudices, to flow is to let go
completely, to drop the baggage of prejudice . . .

Mike continues for another paragraph or so, writing about his
hopes, his fears, his uncertainties, before ending the piece with this
couplet:

creative spirits come with infinite questions
i'm dropping one answer for every thousand inquisitions

Reading over their papers as I key this material into my own text
(to the extent that it is my own), I am struck by how much their
papers *sound* like them. Perhaps I shouldn't be. After all, our writing

is *supposed* to sound like us. At least one would think so. But we know how often it doesn't. Jill's essay is economical in its choice of words, yet says what it needs to say quite strongly nonetheless. Mike's is filled with a sense of wonder and awe, and it embraces its imperfections—misspellings, malapropisms—rather than interrupt itself or pause to get corrected. Bryan's text comes with its own sly smirk, beginning with its title: *Bryan's Ways of Knowing.* He begins by commenting on "humanity's search for a tribe to belong to" and about our "Folk Society Deficiency syndrome." He then asks,

> *Is* the Writing Center a folk society or a tribal community? In a way, I, like many of the people I've talked to, have been searching for such a folk society, a little writing community that is organized tribally, for a long time. And, again like many people, I've grown disenchanted and disillusioned, not finding anything that's truly satisfying.

Bryan then traces his trajectory of failed attempts at schooling, declaring that he was "in and out of college from 1992 to 1997." His withdrawal in 1997 he intended to be "for good," coming on the heels of a stifling film course he'd taken at another institution. In that course, he notes, "We'd been lectured all semester on how every film in the world was racist, sexist and homophobic, from *Star Wars* to *Schindler's List* and beyond." Dissenting opinions, he added, were "not welcome."

Bryan's next paragraph offers a disclaimer of a sort:

> I find it useful at this point to say that no, I'm not anti-New England, or a Republican, or a racist, a sexist, a homophobe or a reactionary who yearns for imaginary good old days. I don't believe anything should be taught the way it's been taught before, really. . . . School has never been anything but something standing between my making up my own mind and my accepting what was being offered as truth.

Here Bryan engages with the readings, which he characterizes as echoing many of these same themes: "Students of all colors, shapes, sizes and economic backgrounds feel alienated by the hegemony we've inherited."

He returns, then, to the film class, in particular to the screening of the film he'd produced, entitled *Rave Chicks:*

> It was basically a chase film through the Oregon District of old Dayton that ended with my friend Emily in a dominatrix outfit stepping out of a church gateway and driving a steel-tipped high heel spike through a rubber duck. It took me forever to properly intercut the skewered duck with images of her laughing face in slow motion, but it was a labor of love. No one got it.

Here I feel pain, and Bryan goes on:

> My professor had some grudging praise but made sure to tell me that my work that semester lacked any kind of social message and didn't talk about anything important, 'like homo-sexuality.' This is a flashbulb memory in my head, one seared onto my gray matter.

What a great image, one that brings me back to feedback, to the responses that students can recall a day or a semester or, as in Bryan's case, years later. These moments make me think before I speak, make me wonder whether what I'm about to write or say will become "a flashbulb memory" for one of my students. They make me very careful.

Bryan then briefly chronicles his arrival at the RIC Writing Center, with Katie, a former tutor (who appears later in this text) as the conduit, encouraging him to try working at the Writing Center. Bryan admits that he had "reservations":

> I'd never found anything resembling a folk society in any college I'd attended or visited in the past 8 years . . . And to become involved with a writing group only to have it turn sour on me was not something I wanted to experience again.

Despite these concerns, he gave the Writing Center a try and "bit [his] tongue and did [his] reading when the readings took a familiar turn." For his efforts, he was rewarded, he writes, with:

A whole folder full of essays I probably would have avoided for fear of fascist association. I have a whole slew of academic terms like intersubjectivity, hidden multiplicity, subjective knowing, connective knowing, and collaborative learning in my head. All of these new tools, given to me as tools and not dogma.

In his concluding paragraph, Bryan reflects on the summer, declaring himself

Tremendously grateful that I kept my mouth shut and took things as they came. I really *like* how this place operates so fluidly. I'm going to like the future conversations we'll have around this table. I'm glad I gave you all a shot, and I'm glad you all gave *me* a shot. I've never been able to sell an agenda, but I can talk to people about writing and listen to what they have to say about their lives. My goodness, what a job.

Like Bryan, Lisa is one of the Writing Center's new tutors, but she has participated in the summer sessions more as I expect Jill did last year—quietly, thoughtfully, a woman of few (spoken) words. When Lisa does give voice to her thoughts, though, her insights make it clear that she really "gets" the work. Although her essay reads in some ways like a solidly-written piece of school, opening with a narrative about learning to write in cursive in the second-grade, the details are vivid and capture Lisa making sense of the material in concrete and specific ways. Several paragraphs into the essay, for example, she recounts a conversation with her teacher, Mrs. Franklin:

As I write my line of little J's, something strikes me as odd. Why does the lower-case "J" need a dot? It is not like the lower-case "I" that can be mistaken for a number 1. The dot does not change the sound of the letter like that funny dash over the "E" in my friend José's name. It must have *some* purpose. I raise my hand. Mrs. Franklin comes to my desk and asks what my question is. I look up at her and say, "What's the dot for?" She looks at me quizzically.

"What do you mean?"

"The dot over the little 'J' . . . What does it do?"

"What do you mean 'What does it do'? That's the way the letter is written. It has a dot."

"Okay," I reply, reluctant to argue any further. I continue making my line of J's, only now, the dots are just a little smaller and just a little lighter.

In her analysis of the exchange, Lisa characterizes Mrs. Franklin's reason as "accurate enough" before going on to consider it as an example of the ways in which a child's curiosity is tamped down by formal education: "In school, we learn that there is always one correct answer, and the teacher's job is to measure our ability to find it."

Donna, also new to the Writing Center this year, did not attend the final meeting/sharing of the essays. In fact, it was several weeks into the fall semester, after much prompting from Meg, before Donna actually turned in a culminating essay. My copy arrived in the mail, from Meg, with absolutely no identifying information: no name, no title, no date or purpose. My attention was drawn immediately, in lieu of these things, to the middle and bottom of the first page, where the word "scary" appeared and was later repeated, centered in the middle of two otherwise blank lines. The essay begins:

I stood looking at the open ocean. I had thoughts of sailing. Exploring the hugeness and enjoying just being. Then fear crept into my fantasy. I wondered what would happen to me if the boat I was sailing started to sink. . . . I would be in ocean life's territory, and there would be a substantial communication gap. Would any fish really care what I was saying?

Scary.

If I thrashed enough, and made a big enough scene in their otherwise tranquil ocean, I might be considered a nuisance and be gobbled up by the inhabitants. Serves me right for attracting so much attention. If only I knew the language, maybe then I wouldn't end up like in the belly of the whale . . . [W]hich marine life would I speak with? Who would want to decipher my attempt at a language and my mad scratches?

Scary.

I think about American Indians on government reservations existing in housing developments. I think of their lives and a language that few care about knowing: a history missing, and a group of people neglected and seldom heard from. I think of the people from different places in the United States, isolated not just by location but by income class, gender, and whom they choose to love. . . .

How does one being help another from being swallowed into the belly of the whale?

Acceptance and education. Compassion and a belief in human rights. Respect for all things living. . . . Being able to assimilate into a culture while keeping personal integrity isn't the simplest task to be given. It's hard enough to live in one's own space, but in a space that clearly belongs to another, or so we're told over and over, the challenge can look and feel insurmountable.

It isn't.

Donna's sole direct reference to any of the readings comes in the second-to-last paragraph, when she mentions hooks as an example of someone who refused to accept the limitations others attempted to impose. Donna then concludes her essay with the following paragraph:

Helping people communicate with pride in a culture that is sometimes hostile toward them based on the way they look and where they came from is a task that requires a willingness to learn as well as to teach. It goes beyond "where there's a will there's a way." It gets down to showing someone they're allowed to have a will. Then helping to guide them, and be guided, part of the way.

JOURNALING

It's quiet in my writing center at the moment. I have arrived early this morning, and the tutors are not yet in. Though I get bored without them when they're gone too long (over the summer or over the long winter breaks), I do love poking around an unoccupied-but-recently-occupied (an hour ago, a day ago, last night) writing center. Those times, I feel like I'm snooping in my host's bathroom cabinet. I walk from station to station. The "Happy Thanksgiving" turkey has been replaced on the Magna Doodle by a Christmas tree fashioned of star stamps. A scrap of an assignment from an Info Systems class missed the garbage can—nothing special, not worthy of comment, but that's the point, isn't it? I wouldn't have seen it had I not seen it this way. A new magnetic-poetry poem has appeared on the side of the filing cabinet:

a void
the languid moon
of a cool winter sky
shine/s through
a shadowed forest
a woman cry/s
ache/ing for what/s
gone
a moment

still time trudge/s on

The old stand-by remains:

Lust after boy/s who cook and iron

I notice Sydney's block print on the white board. She closed last night and left this trace:

We couldn't all be cowboys
So some of us are clowns
Some of us are dancers on the wire
We roam from town to town.

I recognize this as the middle stanza of the Counting Crows' song, "Goodnight, Elizabeth." I erase it and scrawl the next few lines in its place:

I hope that everybody
can find a little flame

Me, I say my prayers and I just light myself on fire
And walk out on the wire once again.

A piece of business is tucked in the upper-left-hand corner of the bulletin board, Carina's reminder that any tutors interested in participating in the Evergreen Network (a program that distributes food and toys to needy families in Bridgeport) need to contact her ASAP. The tutor journal sits closed on the coffee table. I pick it up. No new entries.

Last year, for the first year since I've been directing the Fairfield Writing Center, we had no journal. The tutors didn't seem to miss it. But at the first staff meeting of this year, one of the long-term tutors, Kristy, asked if we could be sure to get a notebook for tutors to write in. Easy enough.

Much has been made of the role of journals for writers. Despite all this, I've never been an avid journaler. They too often feel like certifying mechanisms to me. The explicit directions for journals may be to "reflect" on reading material or to "extend" class discussions, but the implicit expectation is that students will demonstrate mastery of course materials in yet one more way—simply another way for faculty to usurp writing that would otherwise be for the students' eyes only. Toby Fulwiler has co-opted the letter (see "Silent Writing Class" in Heinemann's *A Word to the Wise*) so that he can require his students to pass notes to each other in class. What's left?

Meg and her tutors, however, talk often about the central importance of the Tutor Journal to the life of the RIC Writing Center. The archives at the Writing Center contain years' and years' worth of such journals: large black binders, the date stamped down the side, line the back wall of the Center. Meg rarely writes in these journals herself, and the tutors' journaling hour is a paid non-tutoring hour scheduled weekly. What Meg gets in return (and what I get less of but still some) are playful ruminations on tutoring and life and more. Meg and I began systematically reading through these journals several years ago, as part of a presentation we were giving at the 1997 National Writing Centers Association meeting in Park City, Utah. We were going to talk about the journals as tutor-training devices, demonstrating the ways in which the journals engaged traditional notions of writing center practices. We thought that we would use the RIC journals to illustrate the Center's collaborative foundations and then to explore the tensions between that collaborative basis and the "fix-it shop" expectations of many of our colleagues and students. Very few entries emerged, however, simply spouting the party line about indirection, collaboration, and bringing errant sessions under control. Rather than functioning as a regulatory mechanism, these journal entries were truly generative and incredibly rich in unexpected ways. Here are bits and pieces of a few of the entries Meg and I shared at that NWCA session, a not-quite-dialogue between two former tutors, Katie and Jay.[7]

In her first entry of that semester [Spring 1997], Katie writes:

Let me introduce myself. I'm katie. I like pomegranates,
writing short stories, dead leaves that cover brick sidewalks,
sheep, speaking french, and taking pictures. I hate corporate
america, people who laugh at other people's bad grammar,
and the way my ears get really painfully cold when it's windy.
I also have a tremendous guilt complex and I make a mean
coq au vin, a *really* mean one, downright spiteful.

Into the text are pasted frames from the graphic novel *The Sandman* (which one, I'm not sure), and she asks,

have any of you read
"the sandman"?
it's a comic.
it rules the universe.

She also writes:

Thanks Jay for calling my voice "intriguing." I dreamed the
other night that a wild boar had ripped off your toes. That
dream was a strange place . . .
You know, knowledge isn't really transmitted so much as
generated within us all, so there's no need for old tutors to
"guide" new tutors, like give them our knowledge, because
everyone should be forming her own tutoring philosophies by
now, so if everyone's talking about tutoring you know

everything should be fine. I don't know what's going on, but
from reading the journal (the "big one") I sensed some anxiety
on the part of old tutors that stuff is falling apart. In a technical
sense, yes, the money is gone away, and even people are
going away, but the real tragedy isn't that some older people
have left, but if what left with them is their dedication to tutoring, to talking about it, to making themselves better tutors. It's
an arduous task which does involve a certain amount of intro-
spection, and perhaps everyone doesn't have the time, etc. to
do this, but when we did have a journal hour people were
faced weekly with exploring their processes and we all
learned from that, see you really have to form a philosophy.
Well you don't, but it should be hard *not* to, if the community
is together, writing, reading, responding. at least this is the
theory, and we all know how fickle theories can get.

Um.

That's all.

Love

Katie

Jay's first entry of that semester [February 11, 1997] is entitled "My
Attempt at Relating Milan Kundera to Tutoring":

In eight days I'll be able to booze up on a daily basis. I
think about this frequently.

I hope that, in retrospect, we will consider this journal
(being that it is my first of the semester) as "the journal that
started it all." The ideas and theories I will set forth in this
journal will prove to be revolutionary. In a circular sense,
that is.

Yes, this will be the first journal that will demonstrate my
ability to talk myself in circles about absolutely nothing. You
will read along and think that I am about to go somewhere,
about to make my thetic point, but then I will suddenly bring
my self to a place in which I have already been, often to my
own and to your disappointment. But it is inevitable that we
want to put ourselves in the same situations we have been in

before, so that we might get it right. This is how we recreate ourselves. This is how we get answers.

It's hit or miss. Trial and error. Milan Kundera said that it is impossible for us to know whether we did the right thing in life because "the only rehearsal for life is life itself." So we have microlives, lives within our lives, in which we perpetuate those relationships and situations that we got wrong, until we get them right. But the re-creation is healing only when there is change, variation, in the re-creation.

Beethoven's music, in this sense, must have been a way of healing for him. He begins his fifth symphony with a theme (da da da dum . . . da da da dum) that is used throughout the piece in different forms, re-created and varied. In this way, our lives are symphonies with themes that we are compelled to use throughout in different forms. . . .

This repeated return to where we have been and to what we know is where I began this journal. In tutoring, we always repeat the situation and the relationship of the tutoring session in an attempt to get right what we missed in the last one. Although the only rehearsal for a session is a session itself, we have the opportunity to recreate the experience in the next session, and to change it based on reflecting on the last session. This is how tutoring becomes a theme in one's life, like a motif in a novel or a melody in a Beethoven symphony.

—Jay

I think of Todd. I think of Hendrix.

One reviewer of this manuscript observed that entries like Katie's and Jay's offer evidence that the tutors spend a great deal of time thinking about their own writing, but little evidence that the tutors engage in a similar process about the writing of Writing Center users. In follow-up interviews, I ask the tutors to respond to this reviewer's comment. Bryan takes issue with "the underlying assumption that there is a destination to be reached once we reflect in the journal." Nevertheless, he admits that many of the journal entries do reflect a tutor's preoccupation with his or her own writing. Like all of the tutors with whom I spoke, Bryan characterizes the journal as simply "one more way to have a conversation—sometimes with yourself, sometimes with others." Sarah agrees and adds:

There's a lot of repetition in the journals. When you read them they make you aware of the nature of conversation over and over again. The same issues come up over and over again, written by different people or by the same people. Sometimes you want responses; sometimes you don't. Sometimes you get responses; sometimes you don't. [She stops for a moment before summing up her thoughts.] They allow room.

Katie, writing on the 25th of February:

Creative spaces: the silences of tutoring

The academic world expects us to be creative . . . oddly enough, creativity isn't talked about. It's even discouraged. Memorization of facts and other people's ideas is the name of the game. Maybe this is because it's impossible to teach creativity. It's only possible to give examples of creativity . . . but these are often misleading, and students often take these examples and copy them because copy and repeat is what they've been taught.
    What people really need for creativity is space. [Here Katie leaves several lines blank to illustrate her point.]

Space in a conversation is also what is known as "silence."

[I]'m finding it difficult to describe exactly what happens during the creative process. I may be completely wrong, but I feel it has something to do with the intersection of my personal history and the text . . . my emotional impressions while reading the text . . . what I had eaten that day . . . these are only my general impressions of what the process is. I'm finding it difficult to say, exactly.

The creative part of the process cannot speak to me in words. It cannot explain itself. I think what the creative part of the process wants most is silence.

(What does a sperm have to say to an ovum?)

—Katie

I'm reminded of Trinh Minh-Ha.

Katie writing again, on 2 April 97, shortly after she visited New Mexico State University, where she was planning on getting her master's:

I wonder what teaching will be like. Maybe it will be harder and at the same time easier than tutoring. Maybe it will be tutoring multiplied by fifteen. Maybe I will not teach at all this fall, but grade the papers of people I've never met, a stack of blue books on the desk.

On the highway before Las Cruces there was a fissure in the air, a line of grey dust slanting into the gold sand, sharp and defined, the air was like layers of blue gauze behind it, obscuring the Organ mountains which hung like layers of darker cloth behind. It looked like a storm but it was not a storm. Nothing happened, the air stayed where it was, we drove past it in an hour.

–kd

Jay offering a poem on 8 April 97:

TO ONE WHO TORE HIS PAGE OUT

Often, often before
I've made this awful pilgrimage to one
Who cannot visit me, who tore his page
Out: I come back for more . . .
After I learned his pilgrimage erased,
After so many poems and cigarettes,
A life spent listening quietly for joy,

His words at once took a helpless shape,
Revealing naked bodies seen in cold
Mirrors, harsh lights, imperfect and frustrated—
His pilgrimage at last tore out his song.
(the whispered eyes . . .
    . . . the silent stare of words . . .)

I searched in drawers and boxes, for his face,
And found a black and white photo of him.
I noticed first (I never noticed before)
The pale and modest stripes that lined his shirt.
The precise trails his comb left in his hair.
The heavy greyness in his beard and eyes.
The longing for silence that only comes when feet leave pavement.

I have been thinking about writing and bodies.
Speech-tongues
Writing-hands
Typing fingers
Language is created by bodies, and bodies "speak" many
languages. Whatever a body does says something. The
language of movement and process.
    The languages my body speaks are cultural, the language
of many bodies (the way that it walks with a woman), and
they are also exclusive to my body alone and its experiences
(bodies live in the traditions of their drives, exclusive to
themselves).
    Listen to what you are doing.

Though there are certainly entries which speak only of tutorial
strategies, with little or no direct reference to the tutors' lives (inside
or outside of the writing center) and there are some (though fewer)
entries chronicling daily activities (with no reference to tutoring), I
find myself drawn to entries like these, the ones that move back and
forth with relative ease between academic life (not an oxymoron)
and personal experience. In my own writing I've tried to capture the
revolutionary (in a circular sense) nature of their entries. Perhaps

you are a reader like the one Jay invokes, continually thinking that I am "about to go somewhere, about to make my thetic point," only to find that I've brought you back to some place it seems we've already been. I like Jay's suggestion that "[t]his is how we get answers."

The journal for this academic year is just getting underway as I am drafting this, but already the tutors have penned some intriguing entries:

Bryan Log, Stardate October the 5th, 11:11 a.m.

Greetings . . . I spent the morning tutoring and in-between drawing out birth charts for two friends of mine. I'm pretty much going to leave that astrology book at the Writing Center, as I see various people using it and getting a kick out of it, so that makes me happy. This is a very Venus Cancer way for me to feel. I received a 6-month transit chart for my birthday and today certain things are going on in the celestial breadbasket that are affecting me thus: my sun is square to earth (??) so I have to watch my ego today, my mantra is "put others first." I forget what the other celestial relationships are, but other things to look out for today are overeating and the delusion of loneliness. (i.e. I'm not, but if I feel that way, I can rest assured that it's just a trick of the stars and to transcend it. Presumably through the power of my crazy, crazy ego. Who knows . . .)

I've had a variety of appointments this week. Jim, the regular student whom Donna and I share, had no work on Tuesday and canceled today. Donna talked to him, he seemed pretty sick. We're a bit concerned, as he's had trans-continental girlfriend problems, and that's never good. (or fun).

(I'm having trouble writing this, as Donna and Barbara keep teasing me and distracting me. Grrrr . . . you see, I type with two fingers but can type pretty fast, so it looks funny and sounds weird and always solicits comments. Same thing with my guitar picking. I used to be a very bad student. Who the hell are you to tell me how to play, etc., not that I ever got into that conversation. I'd just roll my eyes and act like a heroin addict—such is the "whatever" coolness of yesteryear.)

[Bryan adds several paragraphs about his tutoring sessions here.]

The sky is gray and getting grayer. There's a great Ringo Starr song called "Blue, Turning Gray, Over You." It's a big band, Sinatra-esque number. Highly recommended. It would be a fitting soundtrack for this afternoon.

Now Donna says from behind me, "Your chocolate coffee makes me nervous." I like chocolate milk in coffee. (Not Yoohoo, though, which is Joanne's confession of the moment.) I ask her why, and she says it's because Rutger Hauer lived on chocolate and coffee in a movie and was disturbingly intense. I tell her it's just part of my winding down process—chocolate, cocaine, cigarettes, nicotine patches, a pot of coffee. (Just kidding, folks, this isn't a sneaking-by-you-confession or anything.) Now everyone's talking it up and laughing. It seems an appropo time to end my journal time.

I leave you with this spontaneous haiku I wrote on the way home yesterday afternoon. I looked over and saw this very attractive girl looking over and then pretending she wasn't, and then looking over. I naturally went "hey, wow, this is nice." Then as I was driving away, I thought, "How ridiculous to assume she was checking me out," which led to:

What a strange thing
For a Leo to think
On the 5th of October.

Jenn spent her journaling hour the week of October 19th combing through the collection of old journals, which is a favorite thing to do, and decided to record some of her favorite quotes from them. Her page is a random collection of quotes, then, from old and current tutors:

"Somehow I don't think we ever get over that incessant questioning of ourselves as tutors. It's enough to drive us insane . . . "   —Meghan, Sept. 16, 1998

"Apple picking together is a fine idea." —Jay, Sept. 17, 1998

"Why do I always feel responsible for other people's feelings, for sheltering them from hurt?" —Meghan, Sept. 28, 1998

"What I'm actually doing, I believe, is slowly giving you all pieces of myself." —Joanne, Nov. 18, 1998

[Jenn concludes her entry with a reference to the Moments of Zen that tutors post on the chalkboard from day to day.]

I like them all, for different reasons . . . They are Writing Center Moments of Zen . . .

By early November, tutors are using the journal to wrestle with their definitions of literacy, in preparation for a proposal to the Northeast Writing Centers Association for its annual meeting. Lisa, one of the new tutors, spends a paragraph describing her definition of literacy, one she deems "more conservative" than the definitions offered by most of the other tutors. Then she breaks, scrawls "moving on" (the only two words written in cursive in her entire entry) and offers this tidbit:

This has been a good week to be Lisa. As of 11:29 p.m. last Tuesday, I am 19 years old (ack! I feel so old. What I wouldn't give to be 6 again.) Also as of that day, I have embarked on a brand-new relationship, so I'm pretty psyched about that. This guy can do a kermit the frog impression like nobody I know. What a catch. Well, that's really all that's been going on. I've only had a couple tutoring sessions this past week . . . nothing really noteworthy went on in those. I guess I'll just wrap it up here! Have a good weekend everyone! ~Lisa

Bryan offers that he too had "an interesting week":

Tutoring sessions all went well. Classes are going well. Besides that, this past week has been all about profound shocks to my Ego structures. It started with Katie, who, through finely crafted argument, let me know that I was wearing no clothes

but out strolling through the kingdom. Then it quickly passed
through Boat Chips, my band in case you didn't know (uhh . . .
http://boatchips.iuma.com) and then to my ex-girlfriend Moira,
with whom I had to negotiate national boundaries for our
newly formed separate kingdoms. All in all, I'm amazed.

Bryan invokes the specter of Katie [the former tutor who recruited
him and the author of the earlier journal entries] to refer to an ongoing email exchange prompted by his five-page journal entry on literacy, an entry in which he questions whether the practice in the
writing center "shouldn't be a bit more regimented" before immediately arguing the opposing side:

But it's not our job. That's what the handouts are for. But
chances are these kids have seen the handouts, and they're
not cutting it on their own. How do you properly mix a sense
of grammar-drilling with a sense of writerly expression? The
eternal WC question, it seems, from reviewing old journals.
Plus . . . there's only so much you can do. We're here as a
resource, and we have to maintain a certain detatchment [sic]
in regards to being blown off, cancelled, not listened to, etc.
People make their own reality, and all we really can do is talk
to them about writing and life, etc.

He goes on for another two pages before admitting:

God, I'm in a grumpy mood. Sorry, folks, maybe I should
take a breather and return in a minute. Okay.

Next page. He takes up the mantle again but abandons it about
halfway down the page in favor of the following delineation:

We should hang a picture of Mr. Spock on the wall and do
whatever he tells us to do in our minds.
We should respect everyone's ideas as if they were
indisputable fact, but we should keep in mind that
"indisputable fact" is what gets us in trouble in the first place.

We should not abandon our own principles and beliefs on writing, life, etc., but we should meditate and revise constantly as to how to appropriately bring these into a tutoring session. The Writing Center should allow for some stumbling on this road, and give positive encouragement to people who start to walk better and better.

We should encourage everyone to express themselves as they see fit but be equally dutiful in reminding people that the very concept of "grades" limits that expression.

We should not silence opinions we don't agree with, no matter how fucked up and ignorant they are, and there should never be a Writing Center curriculum in dealing with the fucked-up-ness and ignorance (ie homophobia, fundamentalism, racism, sexism, etc) of people. "What to do if that stuff comes up" is not an invalid question, of course, but we should keep in mind that we'll never come up with a law or a policy that will wipe out ANY of that stuff. . . .

Same shit, different day.

God wins, we all die.

Thanks for listening, folks.

—Bryan

4

CONCLUSION
Thanks for Listening, Folks

Our honeymoon trip, a fall foliage trek through Connecticut, Massachusetts, and Vermont, included a stop at Mass MoCA, the newly-constructed Museum of Contemporary Arts in Massachusetts. The building was spectacular; the work was uneven; and I spent most of our afternoon there sitting on the stairs watching one performative piece: Tim Hawkinson's *Uberorgan*, "a giant, self-playing reed organ" commissioned by Mass MoCA to fill its largest gallery, some twenty-eight feet from ceiling to floor and 300 feet long. I thought about Trimpin's work as I sat there watching this piece work (or is it play?):

> [T]he gallery and its contents insinuate the chest cavity and internal organs of a very large living organism. The beamed ceiling reads like a ribcage, and the translucent, biomorphic bags encapsulated in orange netting are unknown glands or organs delicately traced with blood vessels. *Uberorgan*'s analogy to body organs continues from its visual to its sonic character. Hawkinson notes that every internal organ has a particular tonal signature, a frequency with which it sympathetically resonates due to its specific shape and density. *Every organism's body is, therefore, a potential concert hall.* (Art Card, Mass MoCa, my emphasis)

Last night, I wrote late in my office, waiting for tutors to gather in the Writing Center for a trek to the Acoustic Café, a coffee bar with an open-mike night on Tuesdays, in celebration of the end of the semester. (I haven't given up!) Kristen, one of the new tutors whom I hadn't seen much this semester—her schedule was frantic and my sabbatical meant that I didn't necessarily see every tutor each week—came in looking for one of the others. We exchanged pleasantries, and she mentioned that Mariann (my sabbatical replacement) had observed her tutoring session the previous night. Apparently, it had been stressful, and Kristen remarked that she had needed "about a half an hour of debriefing" with Mariann when all was said and done. Others were coming in and sessions were going on and I didn't get much more out of Kristen than that. This turned out to be the session already described in chapter one, the evening where the student arrived with an outline generated by her professor, convinced that she must figure out a way to write the paper using the ideas she has been told are her own.

Mariann and I stayed on at the café, after the tutors had gone home, listening to music and poetry and talking between sets about the semester. She offered, without knowing that I had already run into Kristen, to talk about the previous night's session, beginning by characterizing Kristen as having a "gift for teaching" and describing Kristen as "really being able to draw students out."

Mariann described the session as "a real loss of innocence" for Kristen. I recognized that feeling, and my chest tightened at the thought that I could be the occasion, even indirectly, for tutors to experience such a moment. She went on to say that Kristen was "truly horrified" by what she had learned in that session, that Kristen wondered aloud why the writing center couldn't "talk back" to such professors, and she asked me if Kristen had seemed to have settled down at all by the time I saw her. I heard myself answering that she had seemed to, playing the tape of our discussion in my head, with Kristen saying that she "couldn't believe anyone would consider that teaching" and with me off-handedly shaking my head and raising my eyebrows and replying "yeah, I know" while I checked the printer and searched for a student folder and did who-knows-what-else as I surely let her know that I didn't find this occasion horrifying or even mildly surprising and that it was not in fact special to me in any way. Now I have learned that it might have been a defining moment for her—it might have been her Todd—and this is not the role I would have chosen to play. That makes me sad. I caution myself to remember that it is not mine, it is hers and it is the student's; that it is not neatly summed up, it is messy. I hear Nancy and the problem of the turning point; I hear Bryan and his ego-fixation. And I know that I need to get mine out of the way if I'm going to think usefully at all about what happened.

Martin—you remember Martin, our lone male tutor who appeared in chapter one—is a very successful student, an extremely bright student. Martin had pretty significant problems with our staff education class. I watched him, over the course of several weeks, disengaging from the class, until I finally decided it was time to open up a space for him—and others—to comment. When asked about the usefulness of the text, Eleanor Kutz's and Hephzibah Roskelly's *Unquiet Pedagogy*, Martin grinned a bit. I could tell he wanted to talk, and he did: after explaining that he was considering teaching and really had been looking forward to hearing the teaching stories presented in the text, he characterized the Kutz/Roskelly text as "not optimistic enough."

I had no useful response. Optimism? Optimism struck me then, and does now, as not even the appropriate frame for discussion, since optimism seems decidedly outcome-oriented. Optimism is fact-based and, as such, it is rooted in the past. We can be optimistic about future events to the extent that we are able to link them in some way to previous successful outcomes. By contrast, *hope* requires us to anticipate successful outcomes even when we have no reasonable expectation that the future will be any different from the past; we simply believe it may be so. Hope in this way, to quote Ernst Bloch, is "capable of surviving disappointment."

It was an optimistic impulse of a sort that left Todd and me struggling to ignore the static and *focus* instead. It is an optimistic impulse that has tutors imagining a right way and a wrong way for a session to proceed, adhering to writing center dogma about who holds the pen or who reads the paper aloud. I contrast this frame of optimism with the frame of hope offered by Jean Bethke Elshtain, the Laura Spelman Rockefeller Professor of Social and Political Ethics at the Divinity School, University of Chicago: "While optimism proffers guarantees that everything will turn out all right and that all problems are solvable, hope, that great theological virtue, urges us to a different stance, one aware of human sin and shortcoming but aware also of our capacities for stewardship and decency and our openness to grace"

(127). Coming upon Elshtain's work was its own moment of grace for me. I had been struggling with the-trouble-with-optimism question all afternoon and left my office to attend a lecture by Elshtain sponsored by Fairfield's Department of Religious Studies. I went not necessarily because I thought Elshtain's topic, Christianity and Politics, spoke especially to me (though with the 2000 presidential election chaos in full swing, I had perhaps more "hope" than usual) but because the colleague sponsoring the lecture is supportive of me and of my work and it seemed only right to do the same. When Elshtain began her lecture, however, with the question "What does it mean to live in hope?" I was intrigued.

Hope seemed immediately to me to be the appropriate counterpoint to optimism, but I wasn't sure why. What is the difference, really, between hope and optimism? Why does performance, whether on stage with a saxophone or in a tutoring session with a student, seem like a hopeful act, if not necessarily an optimistic one?

Looking back at Mike's self-description—"uncertain of the future but eternally hopeful"—I realize that he too has arrived at this place and is struggling, as I am, to find words for it. Hope, as Mike suggests, contains an element of the future. Though Mike doesn't name this philosophy of his (at least not as far as I know), Bloch has. He calls it "concrete utopia," a philosophy which locates utopia in the material conditions of our existence so that we might look for instances of possible futures hinted at in our daily lives. Concrete utopia, according to Giroux and McLaren, "attempts to locate a possible future within the real" (146). They write, "[Bloch's] ontology of the 'not yet' or 'anagnorisis' (recognition) claims that one can ascertain figural traces of the future in remnants of the past. From such an extraordinary position one is compelled through Bloch's brilliant exegesis of hope to understand reality as fundamentally determined by the future rather than the past" (146).

Those summer RIC staff meetings contained elements of the future. Surely there were more typical moments during those sessions than the ones I recounted in the previous chapter. Surely there are more typical tutors than Bryan or Mike, Katie, Donna, or Jill. But it is not in the typical that our hope resides. It is instead in the glimpse and glimmer of the future that excess provides.

A new semester has begun here at Fairfield, post-sabbatical for me, and many of the faces in the Writing Center are unfamiliar. One face in particular belongs to an "at-risk" student about whom I was alerted by a member of the student support services staff. Chris is a diligent student, an endearing student, but he is academically weak, according to the director's reports. I worked with her to set up an appointment for Chris with Sydney, one of our peer tutors. When Chris and Sydney began their session, Chris's body language suggested that he was anxious: Though he was pleasant, he never met her eyes; his knees and feet turned inward under the table, and he rubbed his hands together nervously as he tried to respond to Sydney's questions. When she asked Chris about his goals for writing, he shook his head as he stared down at the table and said, "I just want to be able to write a paper all by myself."

Ten minutes later, when I passed through the Writing Center on my way to class, I noticed Sydney and Chris writing separately, yet in tandem, each on a purple legal pad. Sydney reported that that was "pretty much all they did" for the rest of the session. That seems like a lot to me.

In his book *Noise: The Political Economy of Music*, Jacques Attali breaks his history of western music and political economy into four stages: Sacrificing, Representation, Repetition, and Composition. When he invokes the term *composition*, Attali is not at all using it in its ordinary literary sense, or even in its ordinary musical sense, both of which might suggest transcription, repression, linearity, and containment. His own definition of composition reads like this: "Inventing new codes, inventing the message at the same time as the language" (134). Of the four codes, composition, according to Attali, is the only one that asks us to actively imagine a future. Attali writes, "Any noise, when two people decide to invest their imaginary and their desire in it, becomes a potential relationship, future order" (143). For the writing center, such imagining involves refusing an identity construction that merely positions the center as a reduplication of the sound of the academy. This is work. This is throwing out the script. But how I love the suggestion that two people make decisions about whether and how to invest themselves in what may appear to be sheer chaos and that those decisions, these investments, create an opportunity for a future, for new relationships, for new ways of being together.

It is striking to realize that the tutors themselves often have difficulty recognizing the significance of moments like the ones Sydney and Chris shared. The occasions they tend to downplay—"That's pretty much all we did"—are the very same occasions that for me are at the core of our work. Their dismissal makes getting at those moments that much harder. Maybe getting at them should be hard. Perhaps it's a place we—directors, scholars, teachers—shouldn't be *allowed* to go. When I interviewed the RIC tutors at the end of the year, I had trouble getting Bryan (who is normally so verbal) to talk about moments of excess in his own tutoring career. He seemed perplexed, sputtering a bit before Meg prompted him: "What about the work you and Joe did?"

"Oh, with the films? Oh, we just watched each others' films." Bryan and Joe, a Korean student, share a mutual interest in avant-garde film. Joe had, in fact, worked on several Korean films that Bryan was familiar with. They watched a couple together; they traded favorite films; they "talked a lot about film," in Bryan's words. He seemed reluctant to elaborate.

I pressed Mike, too, for more on his sessions with Jason, the Korean student he had worked with. Early in his response, he said, "A lot of what we did was just plain old talking. You know, where we both are as people." Specifically, I wanted him to consider the challenges of working with ESL students. To prompt him, I talked about the frustrations of international students who desperately and quickly want to improve their English in light of the added burdens of coursework, evaluation, and sometimes even their professors' expectations. Mike acknowledged these by saying, "Oh, yeah, the ESL stuff. We talk about that when we get to it." Then he got to the heart of his work with Jason: "But using English words is really where his joy is."

When I reflect on what I expected to find as I prepared for my summer at RIC, I realize that I was looking for evidence that Meg had put in place a program that somehow produced a community of tutors who managed to keep their options open. I wanted to find out how she did that, especially since every program that I had seen (including my own) produced a community of tutors who had shut their options down. I needed to figure out how to work toward the former and move away from the latter. The first few sentences of this paragraph sum up pretty well my expectations for that summer, and I am surprised by the Taylorized mechanization of even my own language: the production and management of community, the figuring-out and the working-toward. I hadn't quite let go. I suppose we can't fully let go. But I believe now, and I have seen at RIC, that "[c]ommunity is not a product; it cannot be built or produced. One *experiences* community" (Davis 196).

For Meg, the heart of the summer sessions is contained in a single line that was spoken somewhere around week five or six, during one particularly heated debate. The discussion gained momentum, with people jumping in, talking over each other, trying to get a word in and then finally giving up. Justin, in particular, tried several times to assert a position that, given the general leanings of the group, was likely to be an unpopular one. He sat forward, started to speak, was stopped, started again, was stopped again, and then finally sat back. It was clear that he was no longer going to try to make himself heard. At that moment, Mike jumped into the fray. When he was finally recognized, rather than make his own point (which was sure to be at the opposite end of the political spectrum from Justin's), he looked across the room, lay his open palm on the table, and said, "Justin, what was it you were trying to say?" Davis writes, "It is not in the work but in the 'unworking' that community is exposed, *not in the pulling together but in the brrreaking up* . . . 'Pulling together' doesn't produce community, but c-r-r-r-a-c-king up exposes it" (2000, 196-197).

When Sarah confesses that the summer sessions left her, rather than with a bunch of strategies in her tutoring bag, with the feeling that they had spent the summer "just talking," she is acknowledging the exposition of community in the c-r-r-r-a-c-king up. The sessions leave the tutors not with the sense that everything has magically come together, but with, oddly, the general impression that things have been broken up. While this sensation can be unsettling, it is also strangely freeing.

Back to Hawkinson, to the *Uberorgan*, that "hilarious, enchanting, vast instrument, the one that "'overcomes' the classical pipe organ by subverting its pious grandiosity":

> The grand silliness of the *Uberorgan*, its low-tech sophistication and handmade craftsmanship, its complexity and truly vast scale are all put in the service of a playful, mirthful, even goofy end—the *Uberorgan* laughs at itself, and we smile along with it. The *Uberorgan* welcomes chaos and overcomes organization: its switches render the encoded score gloriously unpredictable and convoluted. (Mass MoCa Art Card)

Even as the summer sessions at RIC were not what I expected, they were still somehow just what I had imagined. The participants took an encoded score—Kenneth Bruffee's "Collaborative Learning" and Paolo Freire's *Pedagogy of the Oppressed* being two notable examples—and rendered it gloriously unpredictable, setting the texts in motion with the pitch of a beast or the jangle of a set of keys. They sought creativity in repetition: What happens when we read *Women's Ways of Knowing* again, knowing what we know *now*? Listening to it with a different set of ears ... in the key provided by these new voices? And they welcomed the chaos that ensued when that repetition didn't turn out quite as planned.

I have not had the opportunity to observe much of the tutoring for which the summer sessions prepared the RIC group, but I have been fortunate enough to have them tutor me on parts of this book. They have now just finished reading a draft of the chapter on the summer sessions, and an email message containing their responses to it was waiting for me in my mailbox this morning. Their notes are brief, but they comment very carefully on my writing. Barbara, for example, begins by highlighting what she liked about the chapter:

> It's so interesting to have witnessed the summer training first hand and to see what things you pick out for your book. I think your take on things was right on.

The last few sentences of her response, however, contain what she calls her "only criticism":

> [I]t left me hanging. It sort of ended but without concluding your point. . . . I was confused by that. Maybe it's me, maybe I missed something, because I like things to be tidy and in a neat little package.

Jill agrees that I seem to have "captured the atmosphere of the summer sessions" before gently suggesting that

> it might be helpful to explain a little why we chose those readings, and what agenda we had in mind before the meetings began. This would provide more of a contrast for when you bring up the scrapping of *Women's Ways*.

She also was confused about the point I was trying to make with the journals.

In the middle of Bryan's note, where he summarizes his experience of reading the chapter and of seeing his own contributions in it, he writes,

> All of the excerpts are great, particularly Donna's, Jay's and Katie's. I miss Donna. She was a great rabble-rouser. We had our different agendas, but I miss talking to her. We never even got a chance to argue.[1]

The tutors will not have the opportunity to respond to all of these concluding thoughts, though their possible comments ring in my head as I write this. I expect Mike might push away from the table for a moment after reading about the *Uberorgan*; Bryan would probably give a wry smile as he kept reading; Jill, Joanne, and Barbara might want more explicit connections made between the *Uberorgan*, my thoughts, and their own contributions to this text. They would all be right on. Like Mike, I was blown away by the relevance of the *Uberorgan* to this book when I sat and watched it that rainy afternoon. Yet now, removed from it in space and time, I am at a loss to articulate its relationship in any insightful, sophisticated way. Like

Barbara, I had hoped that my conclusion might straighten up the text a bit, that I could tie things together in some neat little package and present it to you, The Reader. But every day I listen to a session in the Fairfield Writing Center, or I talk to a tutor about the past/present/future, or I get a journal entry from the RIC group, and I find I want to say just one more thing. And another thing. I don't know how to make it end. I don't know that it does. I seem to be caught in my own feedback loop.

Yesterday, in my staff education course, we talked about rituals for writing, and I confessed that one of mine was to go back and re-read pieces of writing that I really like. So today I settled in with Blitz's and Hurlbert's "If You Have Ghosts." I especially love the ending, where Michael Blitz is recounting the noise from the writing center he heard from his office one afternoon. He writes, "I heard arguments and then laughter—lots of laughter. When I came in I found Ericka, Leana, and Sonya all laughing with tears in their eyes"(92). In the final paragraph of the essay, Michael says,

> The three of them were clearly a safe haven for one another in that moment, and that's what moved me so much. They had told each other important things; they'd laughed out loud not only in amusement but also as an act of caring; in some ways they'd gone beyond the expressed purposes of the writing center to discover at least something maybe each would only have whispered. (92)

Blitz and Hurlbert conclude by remarking, "If we have ghosts, they would be in the after-image of this scene and the occasional questioning voice that wonders why such moments of shared discovery are not at the very center of what we're supposed to be teaching" (92).

I view this last line as a challenge, and I consider this book a partial response.

SECRET SOUNDS

For several months, these next two paragraphs marked the beginning of the draft of this book's conclusion:

Moving into our new house has meant adjusting to a brief but dense commute along Connecticut's I-95 corridor. I don't look forward to it, and I can't imagine I'll ever get used to it, but it has gotten me reacquainted with morning radio. Some programs, like the "Name That Member in the Month of September" contest, are admittedly inauspicious. Others have intrigued me enough to at least silently play along as the exits creep by. One New York station, for example, brought back the old "Secret Sounds" game, where the DJs play a familiar sound, amplified beyond recognition, and invite listeners to call in and guess the sounds. A few samples are guessed very quickly, while others take longer, and I sometimes find that I am listening to the same sound in the afternoon that was being played that morning. One particular sound I heard repeated morning and afternoon for two days—until a listener guessed it on the second afternoon. It was a CD being removed from its jewel-box.

I am not good at this game. I strain to hear what I think might be clues, listening for pitch and timbre, for characteristic noises. The sounds are always familiar to me, their names right at the tip of my tongue, but I can't quite make the connection. I couldn't believe, however that I had failed to recognize the CD jewel-box. I mean, the squeeze of a metal oil-can, okay. (Although it probably means I need to check the chain on my bike.) But a CD case?! I was pretty disappointed in myself. I went home and, when no one was looking, began loosening CDs from their holders, one after another. They all sound *slightly* different, I consoled myself. The pitch, I've discovered, really depends on how tightly the CD fits into the holder: the tighter the fit, the higher the pitch.

In a flurry of final revisions, I deleted the preceding Secret Sounds paragraphs altogether, turned off my computer, and went home. Three days later, I received this email message from Joanne (who had been reading the earlier version of the conclusion):

> p. 164. Are you going to further your section on the CD-jewel box noises and connections? That last paragraph screams "tutoring sessions" and "WC" to me. Things like: straining to hear/listening/characteristic noises/familiar/making a connection/disappointment/slightly different sounds/tighter the fit, higher the pitch.

Great.

I frantically searched through various hard copies of drafts that I'd printed out, twenty pages here or there that had traveled with me to visit family and friends, to interview potential colleagues at MLA. I found an old version containing the Secret Sounds paragraphs and looked at what "scream[ed]" out to Joanne, and I was brought back to my writing about Todd, to my exchange with PC. The straining; the disappointment; the possible connections—some made, some lost.

I did not anticipate, when I had these encounters with Todd and PC, when I began thinking about these encounters or even writing about them, that this would become a book, in the end, about hope. Many of the moments that sent me to write were not narratives that, on first pass, seemed particularly hopeful. In fact, much of what we're met with every day is downright disappointing. The writing center could certainly become about those instances: the colleagues who don't understand what we do, the students who are difficult to engage, the mounds and mounds of administrative work that threaten to bury us each year.

We also know the writing center to be about other things: the colleagues (however few they may be) who actually get it; the student who works diligently with a tutor on a screenplay he's writing just for fun; the tutors who develop into careful, reflective teachers over the course of their years here.

But in the writing center I know most of the time, there exists no such clear demarcation between good moments and bad ones. Much the way Donna understands pain, I understand tutoring: the sessions are what they are. "Good" and "bad" seem to me to be labels that we assign in retrospect, labels that belie the complexity of the work of teaching and learning and writing and being human. Such designations led me to think about Todd as a problem to be solved rather than as a soul to be touched. Since then I've learned that most days in the writing center should be, when you get right down to it, about time spent—time spent with ourselves and time spent with others. And the question then is *How* is that time being spent? How might it be spent differently? Can the present suggest not only how we frame the past (as in, "That was a really baaaad session") but also how we frame the future?

In a write-up of the upcoming exhibition "Dangerous Curves: the Art of the Guitar" at the Brooklyn Museum, Jon Pareles characterizes the guitar as "no longer merely a machine that makes sounds." He writes, "Without playing a note, it is already a bundle of meaning and possibilities" (p. 1). The last several decades of scholarship on writing centers has provided us with rich descriptions of the skills and strategies of writing center practitioners. We have not so self-consciously considered, however, the ways in which the writing center is no longer (was it ever?) merely a machine that makes writers (much less writing). How, without sounding a note, the writing center is already a bundle of meaning and possibilities hinted at, if not entirely contained, in the product.

Pareles attributes at least part of the guitar's enduring popularity to its being "the most personal of instruments," both for its anthropomorphic shape (body, neck, and head) but more for the "intimate treatment" it receives: "Cradled in a player's lap or strapped across the chest, as close as a loved one, it is caressed or abused with both hands, while its vibrations are felt next to the player's heart" (p.1). Pareles's description reminds me of the intimacy of literate acts: a mother's embrace that is soft and warm; the smooth marble library floor cooling the backs of my thighs on a hot summer day; a stinging assignment to the Pumpkin (-head) Reading Group. Students arrive at our doors carrying these memories with them as surely as if they were strapped across their chests, and we feel these vibrations next to our hearts.

We must strain to hear the notes they arrive playing as we engage the harmonics of their tunes. To paraphrase Mike's poignant description of the RIC Writing Center, shot to Meg from across the Atlantic, this is the noise of the writing center I know at this point.

NOTES

NOTES FOR THE INTRODUCTION

1.   Names of students have been changed. Names of tutors are used with their permission.

2.   The suggestion that we "just tutor" has been used on Wcenter as a means of calling for a return to a simpler version of life in the writing center, one unencumbered by politics, administrative concerns, potential conflicts. A life where some idealized tutor and some idealized student sit together and work, free from such constraints. This is of course never the case. I would like to take this opportunity to encourage readers to think again about the use of the term *just*, following Davis, following Lyotard, who calls attention to the word's double entendre: "merely" and "justly." Though Davis notes that the purpose of her project is in fact "to issue a call to 'just ["merely"] laugh'"(9), it is not the purpose of my project to issue a call to "just tutor." Along with Davis, however, I do hope this project urges readers, as it has urged me, to consider what it means to teach justly.

3.   Deleuze writes, "Practice is a set of relays from one theoretical point to another, and theory is a relay from one practice to another" (qtd. in Bouchard 1997, 206).

NOTES FOR CHAPTER ONE

1.   I employ the term "center" as the preferred descriptor for these spaces, though it should be noted that many schools operate writing "labs" and some operate under terms that identify them as neither "clinics" nor "labs" nor "centers."

2.   Pemberton does not actually consider the lab metaphor among the three metaphors he takes up.

3. Other composition theorists have also written about this fledgling field's reliance on the scientific method/s. See, for example, James Berlin, Peter Carino, Neal Lerner, and Elizabeth Boquet.

4. See Nancy Grimm's *Good Intentions: Writing Center Work for Postmodern Times* for a more nuanced consideration of the ways that writing centers function as both regulatory and liberatory mechanisms for discursive practices.

5. Ehrenreich worked as a maid for one of these cleaning services for three weeks as part of the research for this article.

6. Nineteenth century quarantine signs in the United States varied slightly according to illness, but most contained the following general warning: "Keep Out of This House By Order of the Board of Health; Carrier of [insert here], a Communicable Disease." For examples, see the website of the National Library of Medicine [www.ihm.nlm.nih.gov].

7. Here are Haraway's thoughts on blasphemy: "Blasphemy has always seemed to require taking things very seriously. . . . Blasphemy protects one from the moral majority within, while still insisting on the need for community. Blasphemy is not apostasy. Irony is about contradictions that do not resolve into larger wholes, even dialectically, about the tension of holding incompatible things together because both or all are necessary and true. Irony is about humour and serious play" (149).

8. I single out Leahy's article precisely because this piece represents the fullest and most direct articulation of the sense of community in the writing center. Though Leahy's piece was published nearly a decade ago, the assertion of writing center community among writing center staff has not changed. One recent example occurs in the December 2000 Wcenter thread "Being a Tutor."

9. It could be argued (and has been argued) that current writing center philosophy is consistent with, and has been significantly influenced by, feminist pedagogical philosophy. See, especially, Woolbright.

NOTES FOR CHAPTER TWO

1. Here I must thank Derek Owens for pointing me to this source.

2. An exception to this general rule is outlined in Sarah Davis's recent *Writing Lab Newsletter* article, "Something from Nothing: The

Story (I Love to Tell) of the Development of the Writing Lab at
Chowan College."

3. The text of Lerner's refutation is published in the September 2001
    Writing Lab Newsletter.

4. In an endnote to the published version, Lerner also comments on
    several other quantitative studies of writing center effectiveness
    (one of which is Stephen Newmann's, another one of the studies
    Harris cites), charging that the results of these studies are subject
    to similar questions of statistical rigor and validity.

5. At Fairfield, the two processes—tenure and promotion to associate
    professor—are effectively linked.

6. In his end of the year address to faculty (summarized by the
    Secretary of the General Faculty), Fairfield University President
    Aloysius Kelley called this a "challenging year for community rela-
    tions." "Severe limitations", he said, were placed on the use of the
    practice field: "Lights must be removed, the bleachers repositioned,
    and sound levels have been imposed." He also warned that the bat-
    tle was not over as the neighbors were seeking to "impose more
    restrictions" on the planned construction of a lacrosse/soccer field.

7. Of course, Hendrix himself owes a great debt to many musicians,
    perhaps most notably Buddy Guy, who was playing around with the
    tricks Hendrix made famous long before Hendrix was on the scene.

8. The traditional mirroring model for writing center work is an out-
    growth of the Rogerian non-directive model used in counseling. This
    model has tutors "mirror" students' questions back to them, rather
    than encouraging tutors to answer those questions or to engage in
    meaningful dialogue with the students about their concerns.

9. Rafoth directs the writing center at Indiana University of
    Pennsylvania, where I worked as a graduate student. I do hope Ben
    intended the double entendre in this section heading: complicating
    does matter.

NOTES FOR CHAPTER THREE

1. At Fairfield, this course is a semester-long three-credit course.
    Therefore, the references I make to my own staff education assume
    such a model. I am aware, however, that not all writing centers
    educate tutors in such a course. The staff education program at

Rhode Island College, from which most of the data for this chapter was derived, is not a credit-bearing course. Instead, all tutors, beginning and returning, attend weekly sessions for no credit through much of every summer.

2.   The RIC tutors were asked to write brief individual, autobiographical descriptions for the book. These descriptions are reproduced here exactly as they were sent to me.

3.   Meg's description is the result of a round-robin writing activity— i.e., written collectively—by the tutors.

4.   All formal and informal interviews with the tutors and with Meg were conducted between May 2000 and September 2000, with the exception of the follow-up interviews, which were conducted in June 2001. Email correspondence was collected between November 2000 and April 2001.

5.   A copy of this packet of materials from the Summer 2000 workshop is housed in the archives of the RIC Writing Center.

6.   Even the choice of readings grows out of local tutoring situations. Next summer, tutors will be reading *First They Killed My Father* by Laung Ung in response to several moving sessions this past year with Cambodian students.

7.   All journals are housed in the archives of the RIC Writing Center.

NOTES FOR CHAPTER FOUR

1.   Shortly after the beginning of her first semester as a tutor, Donna unfortunately had to quit working at the writing center. Her life challenges proved incompatible with the necessary routine of work in the writing center. Everyone's loss.

REFERENCES

Attali, Jacques. 1996. *Noise: The Political Economy of Music.* Translated by Brian Massumi. *Theory and History of Literature,* vol. 16. Minneapolis: University of Minnesota Press.

Bailey, J. O. 1946. Remedial Composition for Advanced Students. *College English* 8: 145–148.

Belenky, Mary F., Blythe M. Clinchy, Nancy R. Goldberger, and Jill M. Tarule. 1986. *Women's Ways of Knowing: The Developement of Self, Voice, and Mind.* New York: Basics Books (HarperCollins).

Berlin, James. 1987. *Rhetoric and Reality: Writing Instruction in American College, 1900–1985.* Carbondale: Southern Illinois University Press.

Blitz, Michael, and C. Mark Hurlbert. 2000. If You Have Ghosts. In *Stories from the Center: Connecting Narrative and Theory in the Writing Center,* edited by Lynn Craigue Briggs and Meg Woolbright. Urbana: National Council of Teachers of English.

Boquet, Elizabeth. 1999. "Our Little Secret": A History of Writing Centers, Pre-to Post-Open Admissions. *College Composition and Communication* 50: 463–82.

Bouchard, Donald F., ed. 1997. *Language, Counter-memory, Practice: Selected Essays and Interviews by Michel Foucault.* Translated by Donald F. Bouchard and Sherry Simon. Ithaca, NY: Cornell University Press.

Brannon, Lil, and Stephen M. North. 2000. The Uses of the Margins. *The Writing Center Journal* 20:2, 7–12.

Bruffee, Kenneth A. 1984. Peer Tutoring and the "Conversation of Mankind." In *Writing Centers: Theory and Administration,* edited by Gary A. Olson. Urbana: National Council of Teachers of English.

———. 1989. Collaborative Learning and the "Conversation of Mankind." *College English* 46: 635–52.

Carino, Peter. 1992. What Do We Talk About When We Talk About Our Metaphors: A Cultural Critique of Clinic, Lab, and Center. *The Writing Center Journal* 13:1, 31–42.

Davidson, Levette J., and Frederick Sorenson. 1946. The Basic Communications Course. *College English* 8: 83–6.

Davis, D. Diane. 2000. *Breaking Up [at] Totality: A Rhetoric of Laughter.* Carbondale: Southern Illinois University Press.

Davis, Sarah. 2001. Something from Nothing: The Story (I Love to Tell) of the Development of the Writing Lab at Chowan College. *The Writing Lab Newsletter* 25:6, 14–16.

DeCiccio, Albert C., and Joan Mullin. 2000. "From the Editors." *The Writing Center Journal* 20:2, 5.

Deleuze, Gilles. 1994. *Difference and Repetition.* Translated by Paul Patton. New York: Columbia University Press.

Derrida, Jacques. 1978. *Writing and Difference.* Translated by Alan Bass. Chicago: The University of Chicago Press.

Ehrenreich, Barbara. 2000. Maid to Order: The Politics of Other Women's Work. *Harper's*, April, 59–70.

Elbow, Peter. 1981. *Writing With Power: Techniques for Mastering the Writing Process.* New York: Oxford University Press.

Elshtain, Jean Bethke. 2000. *Who Are We?: Critical Reflections and Hopeful Possibilities.* Grand Rapids MI: Eerdmans.

Foucault, Michel. 1973. *The Birth of the Clinic: An Archaeology of Medical Perception.* Translated by A. M. Sheriden Smith. New York: Vintage.

Fulwiler, Toby. 1994. Silent Writing Class. *A Word to the Wise: Heinemann's Newsletter for College English Faculty* 1:1, 3.

Gere, Anne Ruggles. 1987. *Writing Groups: History, Theory, and Implications.* Carbondale: Southern Illinois University Press.

Gillespie, Paula, and Neal Lerner. 2000. *The Allyn and Bacon Guide to Peer Tutoring.* Boston: Allyn and Bacon.

Giroux, Henry A., and Peter McLaren. 1997. Paulo Freire, Postmodernism, and the Utopian Imagination: A Blochian Reading. In *Not Yet: Reconsidering Ernst Bloch*, edited by Jaime Owen Daniel and Tom Moylan. London: Verso.

Grimm, Nancy Maloney. 1999. *Good Intentions: Writing Center Work for Postmodern Times.* Portsmouth, NH: Heinemann-Boynton/Cook.

Haraway, Donna J. 1991. *Simians, Cyborgs, and Women: The Reinvention of Nature.* New York: Routledge.

Harris, Jeanette, and Joyce Kinkead. 1990. An Interview with the Founding Editors of *The Writing Center Journal*. *The Writing Center Journal* 11:1, 3–14.

Harris, Muriel. 2000. Preparing to Sit at the Head Table: Maintaining Writing Center Viability in the Twenty-First Century. *The Writing Center Journal* 20:2, 13–22.

Hatay, Nona. 1995. *Jimi Hendrix: Reflections and Visions*. San Francisco, CA: Pomegranate Artbooks.

Hayles, N. Katherine. 1988. Two Voices, One Channel: Equivocation in Michel Serres. *Substance* 17:3, 3–12.

Kail, Harvey. 2000. Writing Center Work: An Ongoing Challenge. *The Writing Center Journal* 20:2, 25–28.

Kimmelman, Michael. 2000. "The Irrepressible Ragman of Art," *New York Times* 20 September, Sec. 2.

Kutz, Eleanor and Hephzibah Roskelly. 1991. *An Unquiet Pedagogy: Transforming Practice in the English Classroom*. Portsmouth NH: Heinemann-Boynton/Cook.

Leahy, Richard. 1992. Of Writing Centers, Centeredness, and Centrism. *The Writing Center Journal* 13:1, 43–52.

Lerner, Neal. 2001. "Choosing Beans Wisely." *The Writing Lab Newsletter* 26:1, 1-5.

———. 2001. *Reading Writing Center History*. Unpublished Manuscript.

Macauley, William J. Jr. 2000. Setting the Agenda for the Next 30 Minutes. In *A Tutor's Guide: Helping Writers One to One*, edited by Ben Rafoth. Portsmouth, NH: Heinemann/Boynton/Cook.

Marzorati, Gerald. 2000. "Something New," *The New York Times Magazine*, 19 November, 31.

McAndrew, Donald A. and Thomas A. Reigstad. 2001. *Tutoring Writing: A Practical Guide for Conferences*. Portsmouth NH: Heinemann Boynton/Cook.

Meyer, Emily, and Louise Z. Smith. 1987. *The Practical Tutor*. New York: Oxford University Press.

Miller, Susan. 1991. *Textual Carnivals: The Politics of Composition*. Carbondale: Southern Illinois University Press.

Murch, Walter. 2000. "Stretching Sound to Help the Mind See," *New York Times*, 1 October, sec. 2.

Murray, Charles Shaar. 1989. *Crosstown Traffic: Jimi Hendrix and the Rock 'n' Roll Revolution.* New York: St. Martin's.

Newman, Andy. 2000. "Playing Oompah in the Key of Whatever: A Brooklyn Band Marches to a Different Sousaphone," *New York Times,* 29 June, sec. B1.

North, Stephen M. 1984. The Idea of a Writing Center. *College English* 46: 433–46.

Ott, C. Ann, Elizabeth Boquet, and C. Mark Hurlbert. Dinner in the Classroom Restaurant: Sharing a Graduate Seminar. In *Sharing Pedagogies: Students & Teachers Write About Dialogic Practices,* edited by Gail Tayko and John Paul Tassoni. Portsmouth, NH: Heinemann-Boynton/Cook.

Pareles, Jon. 2000. "Dangerous Curves: The Art of the Guitar," *The New York Times,* 12 November, sec. 2.

Pemberton, Michael. 1992. The Prison, The Hospital, and the Madhouse: Redefining Metaphors for the Writing Center. *The Writing Lab Newsletter* 17:1, 11–16.

Rabuck, Donna Fontanarose. 1995. In *Writing Center Perspectives,* edited by Byron L. Stay, Christina Murphy, and Eric H. Hobson. Emmitsburg, MD: National Writing Centers Association Press.

Rafoth, Ben. 2000. *A Tutor's Guide: Helping One to One.* Portsmouth, NH: Heinemann-Boynton/Cook.

Russolo, Luigi. *The Art of Noises.* 1916; reprint translated by Barclay Brown, New York: Pendragon.

Serres, Michel. 1982. The Origin of Language: Biology, Information Theory and Thermodynamics. Rpt. In *The Oxford Literary Review* 5:1/2, 113–24.

Stewart, Barbara. 2000. "Retrieving the Recyclables: Workers Pick Up Where New Yorkers Leave Off," *New York Times,* 27 June, sec. B1.

Strauss, Neil. 2000. "The Sound of Sculpture," *New York Times,* 28 June, sec. B1, p. 5.

Trinh, T. Minh-Ha, 1991. *When the Moon Waxes Red: Representation, Gender and Cultural Politics.* New York: Routledge.

Welch, Nancy. 1997. *Getting Restless: Rethinking Revision in Writing Instruction.* Portsmouth, NH: Heinemann-Boynton/Cook.

———. 1999. Playing with Reality: Writing Centers after the Mirror Stage. *College Composition and Communication* 51: 51–69.

White, Eric Charles. 1991a. Negentropy, Noise, and Emancipatory Thought. In *Chaos and Order: Complex Dynamics in Literature and Science,* edited by Katherine N. Hayles. Chicago: University of Chicago Press.

———. 1991b. Serres's Revaluation of "Chaos." *New Orleans Review* 18: 94–9.

Woolbright, Meg. 1992. The Politics of Tutoring: Feminism Within the Patriarchy. *The Writing Center Journal* 11:2, 13–28.

INDEX

ABOUT THE AUTHOR

Elizabeth Boquet is director of the writing center and associate professor of English at Fairfield University in Fairfield, CT.

Her published work has appeared in scholarly journals and edited collections. For the past six years, she has served as an at-large representative on the Executive Board of the International Writing Centers Association. In the fall of 2002, she will assume the co-editorship (with Neal Lerner) of the *Writing Center Journal*.